OPERRATICS

SELECTED WORKS BY MICHEL LEIRIS

Simulacre (Paris: Galerie Simon, 1925)

Le point cardinal (Paris: Sagittaire, 1927)

Tauromachies (Paris: G. L. Mano, 1938)

Miroir de la Tauromachie (Paris: G. L. Mano, 1938)

Glossaire j'y serre mes gloses (Paris: Galerie Simon, 1939-40)

L'Âge d'Homme (Paris: Gallimard, 1939)

Nuits san suits (Paris: Fontaine, 1945)

Aurora (Paris: Gallilmard, 1946)

André Masson et son univers (with Georges Limbour)
(Geneva: Trois Collines, 1947)

The Prints of Joan Miro (New York: Curt Valentin, 1947)

La Règle du Jeu: Biffures (Paris: Gallimard, 1948)

La Règle du Jeu: Fourbis (Paris: Gallimard, 1955)

La Règle du Jeu: Fibrilles (Paris: Gallimard, 1966)

La Règle du Jeu: Frêle Bruit (Paris: Gallimard, 1968)

Operratiques (Paris: P.O.L, 1992)

OPERRATICS

Michel Leiris

Edited by Jean Jamin
Translated from the French
by Guy Bennett

GREEN INTEGER
KØBENHAVN & LOS ANGELES
2001

GREEN INTEGER BOOKS
Edited by Per Bregne
København/Los Angeles

Distributed in the United States by Consortium Book
Sales and Distribution, 1045 Westgate Drive, Suite 90
Saint Paul, Minnesota 55114-1065

(323) 857-1115/http://www.greeninteger.com

First English Language Edition 2001
English Language Translation ©2001 by Guy Bennett
©1992 by P.O.L éditeur
Published originally as *Operratiques* (Paris: P.O.L, 1992)
Reprinted by agreement with P.O.L through
Le Bureau du Livre Français
Back cover copy ©2001 by Green Integer
All rights reserved.

This work, published as part of the program of aid for publication,
received support from the French Ministry of Foreign Affairs
and the Cultural Service of the French Embassy in the United States.
*Cet ouvrage publié dans le cadre du programme d'aide à la publication
bénéficie du soutien du Ministère des Affaires Etrangères
et du Service Culturel de l'Ambassade de France aux Etats-Unis.*

Design: Per Bregne
Typography: Guy Bennett
Cover: Detail of photograph by Jerry Bauer, ©Jerry Bauer

LIBRARY OF CONGRESS CATALOGING IN PUBLICATION DATA
Leiris, Michel [1901–1990]
Operratics
ISBN: 1-892295-03-2
p. cm — Green Integer 15
1. Title II. Series III. Translator

Contents

NOTES ON THE PRESENT EDITION   11

Titles   17
Eternal Decline   18
What is an Opera?   20
Opera and Drama   23
Opera is Not an Oratorio   25
The Resonant Space   27
Furniture Music   30
Opera and Lyric Poetry   31
Opera and Pataphysics   33
Romantic Opera and Romantic Drama   35
Credibility   37
Transvestites   39
The Fantastic in Opera   41
The Marvelous in Wagner and Verdi   44
The Lively Hell   48
Eroticism in Opera   50
Love Duo – and Something Else…   52
"Committed" Operas   54
Exoticism in Opera   57
Wagner Librettist   59

The Impossible Wagner 61

Wagner's Paradoxical Destiny 62

Nietzsche and Wagner 64

Verism 66

La Villa Puccini 69

Puccini and Schoenberg 72

Discovery of Monteverdi 74

The Marriage of Thetis and Peleus 77

La ninfa fidela 78

Jephta 79

Il mondo della luna 82

Don Giovanni 83

Die Zauberflöte 86

Fidelio 89

Medea 90

Norma 91

The Barber of Seville 93

Lucia di Lammermoor 95

La Traviata 97

Il Trovatore 100

A Model Opera: *Un ballo in maschera* 103

Rienzi 105

Tristan und Isolde 107

Die Meistersinger	108
Parsifal	109
La Belle Hélène	111
La Damnation de Faust	112
Faust	114
Mignon	116
Mefistofele	117
I Pagliacci	119
Ariadne auf Naxos	122
The Woman without a Shadow	124
Pelléas et Mélisande	126
Louise	128
Tosca	130
Madame Butterfly	132
Turandot	133
Andrea Chénier	143
Lulu	145
Moses and Aaron	146
The Three-Penny Opera	148
Mahagonny	151
The Gay Divorcee	153
Porgy and Bess	154
The Medium (film)	155

The Deaf Man's Glance   156
Liang Shanbo and Zhu Yingtai   157
Chinese Opera   160
Voodoo (dances and chants)   164
Greek Karagheuz   167
Operas on Film   170
Period Performances   173
Unaffected Singing   175
Acting in Music   177
Better than Good?   180
Fortunate Coincidences and Gags   182
Opera and Celebration   185
Opera and Bullfighting   188
Opera and Gastronomy   189
Superstars   191
New Genre   202
Monsieur Gaston   204
Hoffmannian Evenings   207
An Opera Evening in San Gimignano   212
At the Casino d'Enghien   214
The Opera of Rome
    at the Caracalla Thermal Baths   216
A Pilgrimage to Mecca   217

Opera and Folklore 220

Art and Life 222

What We Were Looking for So Far Away 224

What I Find in Opera 226

NOTES 227

INDEX 230

Along with his travel and field notebooks, and the Diary that he kept intermittently from 1922 through 1989,[1] *Operratics is one of the major manuscripts that remained unpublished at the death of Michel Leiris, who left it in my care for possible future publication.*

Neither a treatise, nor an essay, nor a chronicle, nor even a little encyclopedia — in spite of the impression created by the titles he gave to each of the fragments that make up this work ("Operas on Film," "Opera and Folklore," "Opera and Bullfighting," "Transvestites," "The Marvelous in Wagner and Verdi," "Verism,"etc.) — Operratics is first foremost a work of personal observations and memories of the opera, which fascinated him from a very early age, as he explained in L'Age d'homme. Not unlike what we might have said of Jean-Paul Sartre, one of his close friends and contemporaries (who was enlivened as Leiris himself was by the imperious desire to be a writer), we could say that Michel Leiris was not the child

[1] [The diary was published by Gallimard in 1992 – GB].

of the libraries *that Sartre was, but rather a* child of the opera, *indeed a* child of the spectacle, *so dominant is the visual aspect of what he both retains from and expects of opera, as he was most likely more attracted by the performance itself than by the music.*

In January of 1959 Michel Leiris began to note his views, impressions and memories of the opera. At more or less the same time he began writing Fibrilles, *the third volume of* La Règle du jeu. *More clearly than in either* Biffures *or* Fourbis, *in* Fibrilles *he speaks of opera not only as an allegory of his presence in the world ("life like an opera"), but also as the organizing principle of this long chapter,* The Proud, the proud…, *which, like Tristan's interrupted melodic flow, runs through and constitutes the whole work, which is divided into exactly four acts that do not lack movements of the crowd and chorus ("Sunday in Peking"), nor a celebration ("Easter in Kumasi"), nor star-crossed lovers, nor even certain* Verist *elements, with the episode of his unsuccessful suicide attempt which, putting Leiris in the position of becoming his own Franco Alfano, condemns him to finish his book after declaring that he himself had wished to "end it all"… Are we to see here a sort of identification with Puccini who, composing* Turandot *and already se-*

riously ill with the condition that was to end in death, supposedly declared upon finishing Liù's suicide scene (Act III): "The opera will be performed incomplete and someone will step out on the stage and say: 'At this point the Maestro died'"?[2] One might think that Fibrilles, and even more so Operratics, *whose longest fragment is dedicated to* Turandot *and which contains the draft of the note that Leiris would add to a new edition of* L'Age d'homme *in 1964, were written at a time when he himself intended to make amends regarding the barb with which, in the latter book, he had struck Puccini's memory, describing him as* "that other piece of trash"...

Operratics, *which we might consider the technical and, in a way,* "harmonic" *(in the musical sense) side of* Fibrilles, *has nevertheless remained unfinished. At least the fragments that compose it, each one embellished with a title and dedicated to a particular theme, have remained in the form of note cards, whose organization and classification represented the raw material of Michel Leiris' books. With the difference, however, that those which were used in* La Règle du jeu *and which were*

2 Franco Alfano will in fact finish *Turandot*.

hardly removed from their more or less natural destination — the wooden or cardboard files in which he kept them — the "slips of paper" making up Operratics *have been brought together and put into order by him in a metal-ring binder, such that they constitute a relatively closed, homogenous and continuous ensemble, which bears witness — were it not for the occasional handwriting — to the "book" status that he gave it.*

Contructed from a juxtaposition of two terms — opera *and* erratic *— which, penetrating one another, constitute a play on words, forming what could be called a "portmanteau word," the title chosen by Michel Leiris places this work under the sign of what he considered to be one of his* "aficiones" *— the other being bullfighting — with, as is fitting, his outbursts and silences, his manias and digressions, his injustices and penances, his interrogations, too: namely, those of a writer for whom all reflection on the opera might well resolve some of the esthetic problems he was facing: among others, those of* presence, *of the* marvelous, *of* modernity *and, more generally, of* language, *which was, in this case, sung.*

The original manuscript of Operratics *(manuscript no. 12) contains 210 128 × 198 mm sheets of graph* paper, held in a black, metal-ring binder that Leiris had kept next to opera libretti and magazines. Written in blue ink, the pages are very clean; in spots, annotations written on a note card or loose sheet of paper were inserted by him; except where noted, in this edition they are transcribed on the bottom of the page, referenced by an asterisk set at the end of the chapter where they were found. Michel Leiris' notes are also composed at the bottom of the page and referenced by an asterisk. My few notes are referenced by numbers and can be found at the end of the work.[3]

Difficult to read words or those that have been restored, as well as my own intercessions in the text appear within brackets [ ].

The brackets used by Michel Leiris in the manuscript have been replaced by braces { }.

The sentences or paragraphs set off by greater than / less than signs < > indicate passages that had been crossed out in pencil by Michel Leiris, a device he frequently used in his manuscripts and in his notes to remind himself that he had, whether taken as such or reworked, used them in another of his published works.

---

3 [My notes also appear at the end of the book, within brackets as here. – GB]

Generally speaking, Michel Leiris' spelling is very consistent, even regarding proper nouns. Written at different dates, these pages occasionally show slight spelling differences in certain performers' names, which I normalized using Oxford Dictionary of Opera.[4]

—J.J.

---

4 [For my part, I deferred to *Kobbe's Opera Book* for the standard English spellings/transliterations of certain opera titles and performers' names. Regarding opera titles: I have given the original language version in those cases where Leiris did, but use the English version when Leiris himself gives the title in French translation, the only exceptions to this rule being those operas whose original, non-French titles are acceptably translated into that language (i.e. *Il Trovatore/ Le Trouvère*), but not into English. – GB]

TITLES

January 25, 1959: *For the amelioration of the operine race.*

Outline for a preface:

Impertinence – or naïveté – of a mere opera lover (neither a musician nor a man of the theater) publishing his views on opera;

the case of this particular opera lover, however, who is a writer and who therefore deals with aesthetic issues that such reflections – though related to an activity that is not his own – could help him resolve;

utility that such reflections – coming from an outsider, a member of the "good public" – could have for specialists.

March 23, 1959
("operratic" = opera + erratic)

ETERNAL DECLINE

One day, as I deplored the declining state of bullfighting, Picasso mocked me, saying that people have always complained that the corrida was in decline, that the bulls of the past had been bigger, more powerful, etc. While bullfighting has admittedly evolved, that doesn't necessarily mean it is in decline (or only in the sense that an art can be termed "in decline" when the incidental supplants the essential: in this case, the increasingly brillant play of the cape and muleta, the death-blow no longer being the climax, but merely the conclusion).

People frequently talk about the decline of opera. But, taking a good look at it, where is this so-called decline? As far as the interpreters are concerned, if they don't sing as well as in the past (which has yet to be proven, of course), they act better and generally have a more acceptable physique. As far as the works are concerned, a great number of more than notable operas has been composed in the first half of the twentieth century: Puccini, Richard Strauss, Debussy, Ravel, Falla, Alban Berg, Kurt Weill, Charpentier, Stravinsky, these names alone bear witness to that fact. There is no doubt that in today's opera the libretto is more important than before; but does that mean the music is any less important? And even if it were, we could see this as an evolution, a displacement of the center of interest, and not a state of decline.

In a letter dating (I believe) from 1867, Verdi already describes a number of problems with the Paris Opera that are still true today.

WHAT IS AN OPERA?

By "opera" I mean any theatrical work whose basic medium is song. A wide variety of genres fall under this definition: opera strictly speaking, comic opera, light opera, operetta, musicals, lyric drama, etc.

An opera might very well have but a single character (cf. Arnold Schoenberg's *Erwartung*), but the character must sing from within the context of a dramatic action. Theoretically, it is difficult to distinguish the single-character opera from the dramatic song (frequently performed in recitals); likewise, there is no solution of continuity between the single-character play and the monologue (Chekhov's *The Ravages of Tobacco* can easily be seen as one or the other). Nevertheless, we clearly leave the monologue – or the dramatic song – for the theatrical work as soon as we have a decor or, at the very least, when the protagonist embodies his character in a more than allusive way and that by his physical appearance (costume included) he appears to have become that character. The action must also be present and not merely reduced to its narration (in this sense *The Ravages of Tobacco* is no monologue but indeed theater since the character does not relate something that has happened to him but is caught in the present of the speech that he is to deliver to the public). If we stick to this criteria, it remains that certain dramatic songs constitute mini operas; for example, the song *The Shadow* that, as a child, I heard sung in the Alhambra by the declamator Georgel: the singer walks on stage dressed as a ruined gambler (black suit, cape, top hat) and, having described how he lost everything but his "shadow" (projected by a spotlight onto the background), decides to drown himself and his faithful companion and rushes off to throw himself in the Seine. But it's obvious that a such a song could not reasonably be considered an "opera." So what's the difference, if not the musical style? Simplistic in the song (with couplets and repeated refrains), the composition of an opera — were it a "minute-opera" — is much more complex. The definition of opera as theater sung is thus insufficient: theater sung, surely, but not sung in any old way; sung, on the contrary, according to a score that has been "composed" rather than being reduced to segments that could be indefinitely repeated.

Certain great ritual events – with protagonists in costume, mimed actions, music and choruses – are *nearly* operas; but they will only be authentic operas if, on the one hand, the singing is not limited to the chorus reduced to the role of commentator (as in Greek tragedy) and if, on the other, the mimed actions are organized into a drama (as opposed to being mere simulacra of activities).

The great ballets with dramatic plots spanning several acts (*Swan Lake,* for example) are sorts of unsung operas.

There are also intermediaries between ballet and opera (Stravinsky's *Mavra,* a mimed comic opera with singers in the orchestra pit), between oratorio and opera (Stravinsky's *Histoire du soldat*).

OPERA AND DRAMA

The considerable importance of incidental music in contemporary theater. It seems that the opera and the drama of today tend to grow more and more alike. Certain works – the *Dreigroschenoper* for example – are somewhat of a hybrid of drama and opera.

The intensely dramatic effects obtained by the eruption of opera in spoken drama, or vice versa:

in *L'Enfant de l'amour* by Henri Bataille, at the end of an act, a phonograph begins to play, singing, "Go ahead, laugh! Clown...," as the curtain falls;

the *parlando* of certain traditional operas (cf. the reading of the letter in the last act of *La Traviata*);

in *Moses and Aaron,* the opposition of the role of Moses which is nearly declaimed to that of Aaron which is performed in held-tenor style, also, the combinations of spoken choruses and sung choruses; see *Turandot* and the screams from the chorus;

in the Peking operas, the typical highly modulated declamation is replaced by song when the characters relate their situations or in moments of great tension.

Dramas that have been eclipsed by the operas drived from them: *Tosca* by Victorien Sardou, *Pelléas et Mélisande* by Maurice Maeterlinck. To a certain extent, you could even say that "Don Juan" is Mozart's *Don Giovanni*. Likewise, *Le Roi s'amuse* seems outdated, contrary to *Rigoletto*.

OPERA IS NOT AN ORATORIO

The odious tendency of a Wieland Wagner to simplify both decor and staging to such a degree that they suggest a sort of symbolism while avoiding a ridiculous, overly literal representation. The absurdity of his *Fidelio* as it was given in Paris: the decor is so abstract that you can't tell the difference between the jail scenes and those that take place outdoors.

From what I've read or heard, his Bayreuth productions are no less disastrous: does he not actually have Brünnhilde's awakening played by a Brünnhilde without a breastplate, thus keeping Siegfried from discovering that, beneath her armor, she has the breasts of a woman?*

* But his staging of *Salome* (given in 1965 at the Paris Opera) shows that Wieland Wagner has changed his ways: grand tragi-comedy played out between a very "sexy" Salome, an ignoble, effeminate Herod, a Herodias with the aura of a femme fatale, a Jokanaan pale as Christ and whose head will not disappear.

The simple solution is to eliminate the problem at hand: avoid the inanity of those great machines of myth or legend. Thus, we forget that opera is lyrical theater and not oratorio.

Immense absurdity: stage an oratorio (cf. *La Damnation de Faust,* most particularly Maurice Béjart's stupid production).

THE RESONANT SPACE

Typical example: the "Miserere" of *Il Trovatore* (the moving song of the soprano on stage while both the tenor's brillant song and the religious-sounding chorus can be heard from the wings). A sort of baroque architecture whose geometry is enveloped in the surrounding luxuriance. The musical use of the very structure of the stage.

With the three orchestras on stage during the finale of the first act of *Don Giovanni* we have something similar.

Verdi's concern for space occasionally leads him to physically divide the stage: Sparafucile's inn (with the famous quartet sung by Maddalena and the Duke within, Gilda and Rigoletto without); the dungeon in the last act of *Aïda* (Aïda and Radames below, Amnéris singing and the priestesses dancing in two opposing styles above); the end of the second act of *Falstaff* (Nanetta and Fenton behind the partition, Falstaff in the laundry basket, the others scattered around the room).

Even in Wagner we find a few rare examples of on-stage orchestra or off-stage singing: the song contest at the Wartburg in *Tannhäuser,* the final procession of the Masters in *Die Meistersinger,* the sailors' dance in *The Flying Dutchman* and in *Tristan,* the bird song in *Siegfried,* "children's voices from the coupola" from *Parsifal.*

To be sure, these two techniques are not characteristic of opera (people speak "off" in ordinary theater and it's also possible to have music on stage), but in opera that they are taken to an extreme.

For successful ensembles in a traditional opera, the capital importance of positioning the singers in space. If it's done properly, it will be visually satisfactory and musically clearer. The obvious necessity for a close collaboration between the stage manager and music director.

Linking the creation of the "resonant space" with the division into "numbers": a clear distinction of the arias, duos, trios, etc., and choruses or large ensembles seems to go hand in hand with a clear spatial distribution the protagonists, as if the temporal compartmentalization called for its spatial counterpart. It is the very same tendency toward more "realism" that pushed for a continuity of musical discourse and rejected the checkerboard (or "windowbox") distribution of the characters on stage.

With the division into "numbers" implying that at such a moment there will be such a number of people on stage, the music in effect predetermines the skeleton of scenic action.

FURNITURE MUSIC

Long before Satie had formulated this notion,[1] did we not already have something of the genre in "overtures," originally preludes performed while the public took its seat?

The same could be said of "interludes," which fulfill the necessity of creating an atmosphere or effectively *furnishing* the timespan linked to a change of decor. The same is true of certain "finales," leading to the ovation of the audience which is at first seated, then standing and preparing to leave.

How, from the "furniture music" that it originally was, the overture gradually became dramatic music: a pot-pourri of themes to be developed, then the actual musical exposition of the argument.

OPERA AND LYRIC POETRY

Desnos: "Had I been able to find it, I would have included in this collection the text of the *Cantata for the Inauguration of the Museum of Man,* for which Darius Milhaud composed the music.[2] It was a step, between the *Fantomas' Complaint* and *The Man Who Lost His Shadow,* toward the goal I set for myself: the opera considered as the most perfect expression possible of lyricism and drama." (Postface of *Fortunes.*)

Aragon: *Bel Canto Chronicles* (collected series of chronicles on poetry, published in *Europe*).

Poet-librettists: Nerval, Catulle Mendès, Hofmannsthal, Limbour, Supervielle and Saint-Pol Roux, author of *Louise.*

In addition, comic librettos by Jarry, Franc-Nohain, Max Jacob.

Bert[old] Brecht has written plays including songs, as well as librettos.

Segalen was to write an *Orpheus* for Debussy.
Tasso's role in the origins of opera.

Rimbaud: "I became a fabulous opera."

Apollinaire, in *Calligrammes*:
"A gentleman in shirt sleeves
Shaves at his window
Singing a little aria he doesn't know very well
The scene is a whole opera."[3]

OPERA AND PATAPHYSICS

Regarding Alfred Jarry's "Kazoo Theater":

> The characters from the libretto, only half fake and funny; their adventures and emotions, more than half false, the displaced atmosphere of these operas in which musical necessity derails any shred of verisimilitude, the cheap quality of the indissolubly real and fake decors that Jarry wanted more synthetic still, now that's a truly, purely pataphysical universe in which, to use a French expression in its full meaning, *l'on se moque du monde.* Jarry's secret idea is that the world we don't make fun of, the world of serious, important people, is essentially no different than the world of puppets and toys. (Roger Shattuck, liminary note for *L'Objet aimé*).

See in *War and Peace* (book II, 5th part, chapters 9 and 10), Natasha at the opera: description of an opera deliberately reduced to point of absurdity through its decomposition into these basic elements of representation.

See also, in the *New Impressions of Africa* ("The Soul of Victor Hugo," pp 295–299), the description of an opera performance seen as a repeating theatrical event.

Verbal comedy in comic opera: the voluble opening in Rossini, for example; the ludicrously broken phrases in Offenbach (which parody the treatment of phrases in grand opera). Meilhac and Halévy point the way to Alfred Jarry, Franc-Nohain, Max Jacob, etc.

ROMANTIC OPERA
AND ROMANTIC DRAMA

The argument could be made that Romantic opera (cf. Verdi) has held up better than Romantic drama (cf. Hugo). This is probably because, compared to spoken language (in spite of the magic of verse), musical language more successfully tones down the excessive and unlikely aspects of Romantic plots. In sum, it seems that lyrical theater was saved by the additional theatrical convention of speech set to music.

The techniques of traditional opera – the division into numbers, alternating soli, duos, ensembles, etc. – are essentially means of *distancing,* in the Brechtian sense.

...Opera's principal charm – which is generally unrecognized yet which keeps it standing among the ruins of other types of theater – is that nowhere is convention more forced or more unnatural. Indeed, what

could be less natural than a conspirator call-
ing for silence by singing at the top of his
lungs, or a grieving woman expressing her
despair while doing cabrioles… (Théophile
Gautier, *History of Dramatic Art in France Over
the Past Twenty-Five Years,* Paris, Hetzel ed.,
1858—1859, 6 vol.).

CREDIBILITY

What is generally accepted in many traditional operas, because the division into "numbers" (recitatives alternating with arias and ensembles) constantly reminds us that we are dealing with music supported by a drama, is more difficult to accept in modern opera (which, since Wagner, tends toward drama set to music, consisting of continuous lyrical declamation): a paunchy Manrico, for example, is easier to take than an over-the-hill Pelléas; that's because the one is a singer acting and the other an actor singing.

From this point of view, Berg was right on target with *Wozzeck,* all of whose characters could be anybody: an ugly Marie is only more touching; that Wozzeck be obese or bony or that he look like an idiot is not important because he's a "poor guy," not a "hero."

However, this type of difficulty is not characteristic of modern operas alone. In *Orphée* and *Don Giovanni* for example, precisely because they are "myths" and not simple love stories, the physical short-comings of those who play the heros cannot be tolerated.

TRANSVESTITES

Yet another challenge in the staging of certain operas, now that cinema has taught us to be more demanding about the physical appearance of the characters presented to us. Asking a woman to sing, act and not appear ridiculous dressed as a man is just about asking the impossible. Still, a few can manage it: Marisa Morel and Lore Wissman* as Chérubin (the first gracious and mischievous, the second vibrant from head to toe as a future Faublas or Dolmancé), Gré Brouwenstijn as Léonore in *Fidelio*. I myself would shudder with delight to see Renata Tebaldi, whom I so admire, dressed as the rider in the second act of *The Force of Destiny*, and I recall a Sena Jurinac (a pretty woman who sings wonderfully) grotesque as Chérubin.

Does this mean the transvestite should be banished from modern opera? I don't think so, for we would be losing an extremely seductive element

* And, in particular, Sylvia Stahlmann of the Frankfurt Opera!

when – with a little luck – it is successfully achieved.

Is it a perverse charm, rooted in sexuality, or an attraction that stems from the fact that with the transvestite we see, expressed in black and white, the very essence of theater: living beings made into something other than what they are?

A transvestite is more acceptable in opera than in pure theater for, here as well, the music blurs the masquerade.

Positive transvestites (*i.e.,* transvestite performers) in a work with disguises:

Chérubin in *The Marriage of Figaro* (Chérubin is himself disguised in the second and third acts, then there's the general masquerade at the end);

Oscar in *Un ballo in maschera* (disguises of the king, the courtisans and the page himself going to the witch's house; Amelia covered with a veil in the midst of conspirators in stone gray cloaks; masks and dominos – including that of the page – for the final "costume ball");

Octavian in the *Rosenkavalier* (disguised as a girl and the characters with grotesque masks in the last act);

Léonore disguised in *Fidelio.*

THE FANTASTIC IN OPERA

To say nothing of operas that could be called "fantastic" because that's their essential quality (*Der Freischütz, Les Contes d'Hoffmann*), nor even of those make use of great, legendary themes (the murderous statue in *Don Giovanni,* the pact with the devil in the various *Fausts* and *Mefistofele,* the accursed vagabond in *The Flying Dutchman*), a mere glance at the libretti of the most famous operas clearly demonstrates that the fantastic is one of the dramatic forces most frequently used by the makers of operas.

The efficient curse: that of Monterone in *Rigoletto,* those of the father then of the Padre Guardiano in *La Forza del destino.*

The ill omen: the soothsayers in *Un ballo in maschera* and *La Forza del destino,* the aria of the cards in *Carmen,** Herod saying in *Salome*: "I have slipped on some blood…".

---

* The theme of cards as instruments of tragedy is also found

True or false apparitions: *Robert le Diable, La Dame blanche,* Charles v in *Don Carlos,* Titania and the imps in the last act of *Falstaff,* the ghosts of executed suitors in *Turandot.*

Love potions, narcotics and poisons: the potion in *Tristan and Isolde, Romeo and Juliette, Mireille, Gioconda,* Bess lost to drugs in *Porgy and Bess.*

Madness: *I Puritane, Nabucco, Lucia di Lammermoor, Mignon*; the hallucinations of *Boris Godounov,* the delirium of *Wozzeck,* etc.

Somnambulism and hypnotism: Bellini's *La Somnambula,* Menotti's *The Medium.*

Hoffmann, that great specialist of the fantastic, wrote "Fantasies in the manner of Jacques Callot." And we find over and over again in Verdi a picturesque quality recalling Jacques Callot: Sparafucile and his sister Maddalena in *Rigoletto,* the Bohemians of *Il Trovatore,* the soldiers and bawdy women in *La Forza del destino* (whose resemblance to

---

in *La Traviata* and in *La Fanciulla del West* as well as in *The Queen of Spades,* of course.

"Mother Courage" should be emphasized), Falstaff and his partners in debauchery.

The frequency of fantastic or related themes shows the point to which opera, even modern opera, is imbued with Romanticism. Another example: Stravinsky's *The Rake's Progress* and his *L'Histoire du Soldat* (if this non-sung work could in fact be considered opera).

The fantastic intervenes in other modern operas as well: in addition to Busoni's *Il dottore Faust,* a truly fantastic opera, see *Turandot* (where we hear and see a chorus of phantoms), *Lulu* (with Jack the Ripper as a nearly supernatural character), *Bolivar* (the female apparition at the end), *The Turn of the Screw*, Malipiero's *Fable du fils changé* based on a libretto by Pirandello, etc.

Another element related to the fantastic, the "daydream," the motive of so many great arias (cf. in *Don Carlos,* the aria of Philippe II, coincidentally very close to the first daydream of Boris Godounov, which announces his future madness).

THE MARVELOUS IN WAGNER AND VERDI

The magical side of the former – in the tradition advocated by Hoffmann for the Romantic opera (see the *Kreisleriana*) – is reduced in Verdi to the intrusion of the supernatural in the destiny of the individual: for example, Monterone's curse on Rigoletto (the cause of the misfortune leading Sparafucile to kill Gilda who is disguised as a man), the father's curse in *La Forza del destino* (the first in a series of evil spells: the Bohemian girl's evil prediction to the brother, as well as the Padre Guardiano's curse on those who violate the sanctuary of the heroine), the evil prediction of the sorceress (consulted in jest) in *Un ballo in maschera* (in which the friend, named by the voice of fate, becomes the assassin of his friend), etc. In *Giovanna d'Arco*, the theme of voices is combined with that of the father's curse, Verdi's apparent predeliction for the notion of "ill-fortune," an evil prediction or curse, a notion evoking the "jettatura" so common in Italy. The fairy world itself never appears, except in the form of a masquerade or carnival, as in the last act of *Falstaff*.

How Mozart stands at the crossroads of these two types of marvelous: the fairy world (*Die Zauberflöte,* German opera), the real world visited by a fearsome, supernatural intruder (*Don Giovanni,* Italian opera).

The Wagnerian marvelous is never presented as the breaking of the rules of the real world for his entire work is bathed in a mythic or legendary atmosphere. Wagnerian heros are either gods or fated individuals, never mere human beings accidentally attracting misfortune to themselves.

To drink a love potion as Tristan does is to obey one's destiny, not to inadvertently unleash the "forces of destiny." While Elsa cannot not ask Lohengrin his name, Don Giovanni could very well refrain from inviting the statue to dinner. In *Lohengrin,* however, Ortude's sorcery is indeed a fantastic element (applied nevertheless to the fairytale theme of the prince turned into a swan) and, in *The Flying Dutchman,* the fantastic is the chief motivating force (the intrusion of an accursed, evil character who troubles honest, simple people, so that here there is indeed the conjunction of two distinct worlds, which are distinguished musically as well – the only example of this type to be found in Wagner, even though it is noteworthy that he is treating a folkloric legend whose hero, who exists outside of time, is to a certain degree a "fairytale" character).

The Wagnerian opera is in the tradition of the "Romantic opera" as defined by Hoffmann ("The poet and the composer," in *Kreisleriana,* trans. Albert Béguin, Paris, Gallimard, 1949). According to Hoffmann, the "Romantic" opera contrasts with both the "tragic" opera (cf. Glück and Piccinni) and the *opera buffa* (with its interventions of the "fantastic," that is, the "intrusion of eccentricity in ordinary life"), a genre in which the Italians excel.

The height of the theatrical marvelous in Wagner:

Siegfried discovering Brünnhilde's feminity by removing her breastplate.

Flops (because they are unbelievable):

Isolde's potion (*called* but not *shown* to be a love and death potion);

the miracle of the blood in the Graal of the last act of *Parsifal* (because it is well known that the miracle here is a false one).

THE LIVELY HELL

Throughout his work, Verdi frequently wrote in a light-hearted style, as if he wished to set up a Romantic – and, perhaps, Christian – contrast between the light and the serious, the cheerful and the sad, as if he occasionally even wished to give joyous expression to something evil (precisely because it is too joyous).

For example, the dance music in the first act of *Rigoletto* and in the last act of the *Ballo in maschera* (justified in both cases by a ball), the Orpheonic aspect of the fiendish voices and their accompaniment (heard in the wings) in *Giovanna d'Arco,* the (Offenbachian) comic-opera style of the page's role in *Un ballo in maschera* (a role both evil and impulsive since all of the catastrophes are inadvertently due to this reverse "deux ex machina"), the chorus of the Fatted Ox heard from the wings in the last act of *La Traviata* shortly before the death of Violetta.

Likewise, in *Porgy and Bess,* Gershwin uses a jazz style for Bess's corruptor (who is in fact a jazz musician).

The same romantic idea of the lively hell may well be at the base of the musical jokes (quotes from arias of the time and from Mozart himself) in the last act of *Don Giovanni.*

The theme of evil laughter in *Un ballo in maschera:* the governor (or monarch) creates his own misfortune by laughing at the witch's prophecy, the ironic laughter of the conspirators induce the deceived (or at least he thinks he is) friend to join them. In addition, the light-heartedness of the page Oscar.*

---

* "I find our opera too monotonous, so much so that today I would refuse to write on subjects like *Nabusco, Foscari,* etc. They present situations of great interest, but they lack variety. There is but a single thread, sublime, perhaps, but always the same. Let me be clear: Tasso's poem is perhaps better, but I prefer the Arioste by far. For the same reason, I prefer Shakespeare to all playwrights, including the Greeks" (Letter from Verdi to Antonio Somma, Sant'Agata, April 22, 1853 – in *L'Arc,* no. 81, "Verdi," 5–6).[4]

49

EROTICISM IN OPERA

Eroticism seems to be used in "grand opera" more for its flashy appeal than for any other reason. The Folies-Bergère aspect of scenes such as those of the Venusberg in *Tannhäuser,* the Walpurgis Night in *Faust,* the lascivious dances of the slaves, priestesses or captives in *Aïda,* the bacchanale around the Golden Calf in *Moses and Aaron.* But it all remains rather innocent and, in the end, is little more than Châtelet for adults.

Nevertheless, the occasional opera is tinged with eroticism from beginning to end: Strauss's *Salome* and *Elektra,* for example, or Alban Berg's *Lulu.* The *Rosenkavalier* — indeed *The Marriage of Figaro* — are marked by an underlying eroticism, at the very least.

Operas also occasionally hit an erotic "high point" without necessarily being erotic works: *Siegfried,* for example, with the awakening of Brünnhilde whose breasts are (in theory) revealed when her breastplate is removed.

Given opera's "festive" character (more pronounced than in other forms of theatrical representation), one would expect eroticism to play a greater role. Yet this is not the case: in opera, as in other forms of entertainment and other arts in general, eroticism remains a special element. In the nineteenth century – which can be considered opera's "great century," when opera was truly a festive occasion since men attended in evening dress and women in low-cut gowns – it was not necessary to present eroticism on the stage, since it was physically present in the hall… Moreover: although there is no nineteenth-century opera in which love plays no role whatsoever (it intervenes even in *Boris Godounov* in the Polish episode and in *Parsifal* with both Kundry and the flower girls), love was so disembodied that physically laughable, repulsive performers were tolerated in the roles of lovers.

LOVE DUO – AND SOMETHING ELSE...

We are only too ready to believe that – with the rare exception – 19th century opera is little more than a love duo filled out with a few other episodes. The importance of certain political themes (in keeping with the liberalism of a good part of the bourgeoisie of the time) in the libretti of many traditional operas is generally underestimated. For example, I recall the thing that caught my parents' attention in the scenario of the *Huguenots*: the noble attitude of the Duke of Nevers, a Catholic lord who rises up against the Saint-Barthélemy (a role sung, in their day, by the greatest baritones); conversely, the cruel loyalism of the Count of Saint-Bris, one of the architects of the massacre; furthermore, the rough courage and unshakable faith of the old Protestant Marcel (a bass role like that of Saint-Bris). As for the love of the two protagonists (soprano and tenor), both of whom perished as victims of the fanaticism, it was all the more moving as it brought together a Protestant man and a Catholic woman.

Contrary to certain commonplace ideas regarding the contribution of Wagner and Debussy, we observe that with *Tristan* — which so often contrasts with the so-called silliness of traditional opera — and with *Pelléas* — which supposedly broke with 19th century opera — we have the most perfect examples of operas virtually reduced to being nothing more than love duos.

"COMMITTED" OPERAS

So many of Verdi's works can be seen as such: the "risorgimentiste" meaning given to several of his operas by his contemporaries:

Le Roi s'amuse having become *Rigoletto,* as a result of Austrian censorship;

the anticlericalism of *Aïda* (the terrible role of the priests, who call for the Ethiopian prisoners' execution, prove to be merciless when it comes to Radames and, in the last act, triumph in the solar world up above while Radames and Aïda choke in the nocturnal world down below);

Don Carlos: the terror of the Inquisition, Spanish oppression of the Flemish people and decision of the two friends – Carlos and Rodrigo – to act as liberators, the tyrannical character of Philippe II and his solitude as a ruler (his famous aria, as type of royal soliloquy, should be compared to Egisthe's monologue: "I come, I go, I can shout very loud…!" in Sartre's *Les Mouches*; to be compared also – to a certain degree – to Nerval's poem

"Rêverie de Charles VI," and to what de Chirico's painting *Le Mauvais Génie d'un roi* evokes: the timorous, cloistered kings are bored, wrapped in their long cloaks, their scepters pointed into the air to thwart the lightning, behind a fence of lances).

Wagner's Messianic side: the denunciation of the evil character of gold in the *The Ring of the Nibelung,* the affirmation of the supremacy of passion in *Tristan,* the manifesto of a new esthetic in *Die Meistersinger,* the apology of purity in *Parsifal* (ignoble aspects of this work, where stones are thrown at all those who are not "pure": Kundry dies like a dog on the altar steps; Amfortas is punished for fornication and is sharply rebuffed when he complains, before his father's coffin, of his misfortune and the suffering caused by his wound; Parsifal "a simple, pure man who follows his heart," is comparable to the s.s. brought up in the Ordenburger under Hitler).

Boris Godounov as drama of the Russian people.

The topicality of *Tosca* (the theme of police repression and torture), of *Fidelio* (prison).

An opera to be written: *L'Affaire Dreyfus* (Colonel Henry's monologue before his suicide would make a beautiful scene; popular scenes in street cafés with people arguing vehemently; Paul Déroulède and the chorus of patriots; touching role of Mme Dreyfus doing what she can to save her husband; possibly, huge scene of military degradation; etc.). {Since this note, Nabokov has written a *Death of Rasputin*}.

It seems that Auber's *La Muette de Portici* sparked a political revolution in Brussels.

EXOTICISM IN OPERA

After *Les Indes galantes* and the "*turqueries*" of Mozart and Rossini, there are many examples of operas that take place in an exotic setting, which is more or less exploited musically:

L'Africaine and *Lakmé* (India);

Aïda (Egypt); *Salammbô* (Carthage);

Les Pêcheurs de perles (Ceylon);

Madame Butterfly (Japan);

Turandot (China).

Note also the Spanish exoticism of *Carmen* (prefigured by the first scene of the Princess Eboli in *Don Carlos*), the Sicilian exoticism of *Cavalleria rusticana,* the "pioneer" and "redskin" exoticism of *La Fanciulla del West,* the Latin American exoticism of *Bolivar.*

In China I saw a *Song of the Steppe* whose action was set near Tibet and whose score apparently called for popular local themes (as if orchestrated by a Cilea or Alfano, so I thought).

To my knowledge, Africa has not yet been used

and the only Blacks to have had the honor of an opera scene are, aside from the Monostatos of *The Magic Flute* and the "Moor" *Otello,* the black slaves of *Bolivar* and the Southern American blacks in *Porgy and Bess.* I nearly forgot the Ethopian Aïda, as well as the black witch (who was Scandinavian in the original libretto) in *Un ballo in maschera* (and, as another of Verdi's exotic characters, the hero of *La Forza del destino* who is a half-breed Inca).

Strauss's *Salomé* is perhaps the only great opera based on a Biblical story in which there is exotic intent. Nothing of the sort in Méhul's *Joseph,* Verdi's *Nabucco,* nor in Schoenberg's *Moses and Aaron.*

WAGNER LIBRETTIST

Did Wagner – who strove for the complete opera from a libretto endowed with true poetic value and philosophical import – not actually arrive (except in *Tristan* where the old legend, virtually unchanged and very simple besides, carries the action) at librettos which were more awful than most and which stuck him, from the musical point of view, with the necessity of commenting all the while on on his abundant, high-flown language?

Especially regarding *Parsifal,* was it not an aberration to represent a ritual on the pretext of creating sacred theater? If theatrical representation in itself is a ritual, staging a simulacrum of a ritual is exactly what you shouldn't do, for you can't get caught up in the *reality* of a ritual if in the context of this ritual you are openly shown a ritual whose theatrical nature cannot be denied.

If the *Zauberflöte* is, like *Parsifal,* an initiatory opera, at least it is presented as a simple fairytale world.

In the current state of things, can myths be staged without ironic intent? In the *Zauberflöte* — and, also, in *Don Giovanni* — the comedy (which represents this irony) makes the myth believable.

Attaching undue importance to a long, complicated text, Wagner takes the exact opposite path to that which, in the words of one of his characters (Ludwig in [*illegible name*]), Hoffmann recommended to the opera librettist: "…his chief effort must in all necessity aim at ordering the scenes in such a way that the subject unfolds, clear and limpid, before the eyes of the spectator. The spectator must be able to get an idea of the plot based on what he has seen, almost without understanding a single word of the text." Puccini said more or less the same thing regarding *The Girl of the Golden West*.

THE IMPOSSIBLE WAGNER

More than anyone else, Wagner set nearly impossible performance standards for himself: the *The Ring of the Nibelung,* for example, would require interpreters "as beautiful as gods" (while Wagnerian singers, who need considerable vocal means, are more often than not of monstruous size), and should have costumes and sets created by an artist of exceptional taste and imagination, as this series of "total operas" not only brings into play elements of the fantastic which are taken much too seriously to be anything but ridiculous, but also has to attain from all points of view the level of the sublime to which the listener/spectator is expressly invited to expect.

WAGNER'S PARADOXICAL DESTINY

He wanted to create an opera that was more than a pretext to music. In fact, if his operas still move us it is generally through the magic of their music.

He believed, through the deliberate use of the *leitmotiv,* he could give opera both a musical and a symbolic structure. In fact, for most contemporary listeners, Wagnerian *leitmotive* only make sense as music and, when their significance is recognized, it takes on the annoying familiarity of theme music of a radio show.

The step-father [?] of racist [Houston Stewart] Chamberlain has today been betrayed by his own blood, since we see his grandson Wieland Wagner – with his minimalist productions – go against the idea of opera as total theater.

The pure bard of the pure *Parsifal* – the crowning achievement of Wagnerian opera – was found dead, the victim of an ancillary fellation, at the Vendramin-Calergi Palace (which happens to be

today, in Venice, the seat of the Winter Casino, alternating with the Summer Casino on the Lido).

NIETZSCHE AND WAGNER

Today, at least some of Nietzsche's indictments of Wagner betray the worst reactionary spirit: the "morbid" character of his music, his desire to create a theater for the people.

It is also funny to think that Wagner was among the very first to like *Carmen* and that it's thanks to him that Nietzsche came to know it.

What in Nietzsche seems to be the complete opposite of Wagner is his *aphoristic* mode of expression: successive sparks, rather than a long flow. This rejection of discourse makes Nietzsche a "modern," while Wagner – with his grandiose, fluid lyricism – can only be considered a Romantic. Is not the substitution of a continuous melody for the traditional division into numbers essentially anti-aphoristic? Anticlassical even (and, if you like, "morbid" in the sense that it effaces structure).

Creating theater for the people in which the old Germanic myths come to life, does this not anticipate national socialism? On the other hand, such bad habits are excluded by Nietzsche's aristocratism.

VERISM

The Italian counterpart of French Naturalism, Italian "Verism" – promoted by Sicilian Giovanni Verga, author of the play from which the libretto of *Cavalleria rusticana* was taken – is not exactly "Naturalism" (at least not in the play by Verga) for the reality in question is a privileged reality: a tragedy borrowed from everyday life, from trivial events (such as those reproduced in color on the covers of the *Corriere della sera*).

Verism (it seems) is born when the bourgeoisie begins to take interest in the people which it can only consider in picturesque terms, so that it will inevitably lead to a "behavioral study" focusing on the local color of the peasantry which has remained primitive, the deeds and acts of the underworld, and the violent, extreme actions perpetrated by the common people.

Does the historical opera, which preceded the Verist opera, respond to the era in which the bourgeoisie was preparing, carrying out or had just finished (which is the case in France with Meyerbeer's operas) its revolution against the tyrants, so that, ideologically, the dominant tone is one of liberalism, as so many 19th century librettos would indicate? In a movement analoguous to that of Victor Hugo, for example, going from *Notre-Dame de Paris* to *Les Misérables* — that is, from a historical realism based in the past to one based on the contemporary era which is taking on its own social problems — does Verist opera come about when the question of Socialism is first asked?

Of the first Verist operas set among the peasantry, there are those like Racine's *Bajazet,* where temporal distance — the rule in tragedy — is replaced by spatial distance, and exoticism is substituted for the archaism of the historical opera.

It is only with *Louise* that opera will come to total Naturalism: no exoticism (as opposed to *Cavalleria rusticana* and other peasant dramas), no archaism (as opposed to *La Bohème* whose action benefits from a slight distance) and less "bel canto" than in *La Traviata* which, set in the Paris of the time, announces Verist opera or, at the very least, breaks with historical opera. *Louise,* which appeals to no privileged reality and limits itself to staging the daily life of the little people, could be called a "populist opera."

The Verist side of *Wozzeck,* at the very least regarding the text: Büchner drew his inspiration from a trivial event. That *Wozzeck* is, without a doubt, the greatest opera of our time comes perhaps from that: the treatment according to very strict musical forms (as Berg himself explained) of a drama which is both Verist and rich in philosophical resonances; the work finally appears as an extraordinarily condensed synthesis of Classicism, Romanticism and Naturalism.

LA VILLA PUCCINI

On September 16, 1958, the Massons, Z[ette] and I go from Montecatini Terme to Torre del Lago (near Viareggio) to visit Puccini's villa, which is today a museum.[5]

On the square, between the entrance to the master's house and the lake, stands a bronze statue of Puccini surrounded by banks of flowers. The pedestal is very low, so that the life-size Puccini, wearing a fedora and a turned-up raglan collar, seems to stand among the passersby. A number of postcard stands and café-restaurants with narrow wooden terraces give on the lake.

A lagoon landscape, softly lit and a little Chinese (after all, this is where *Butterfly* was composed). Pleasure boats, small craft and motorized canoes captained by duck hunters (on one of them a dog stands watch on the prow).

The villa is decorated in half-traditional Italian villa (no joke), half modern-style style (with very Mucha-like figures). In the studio, the desk (on which we see a bottle of quinine and packs of letters in cellophane); at a right angle from this desk, the upright piano, with a swiveling chair that gives access to both the keyboard and the desk. From this room, down a short arched passageway to the right of the piano, you arrive at the funerary chapel. The master's casket is just behind the piano (as the museum attendant told us as she pointed at the instrument); above the master's casket, that of his son Antonio and, on top, that of Elvira, Giacomo's wife. On this wall (the left wall in relation to the altar at the back), a high relief sculpture depicting music in mourning. On the right wall, another sculpted feminine figure representing music which is eternally reborn (or rather, music as a means to immortality or eternal rebirth for the composer). You can also visit a vestibule containing several pairs of Puccini's shoes, his hunting raincoat and various objects including a huge camera. Finally, you enter a salon which, like the other rooms, contains numerous souvenirs: signed photos, posters, various knick-knacks. An old woman, whom we see momentarily with our guide, tells us that she worked as a maid in Puccini's house for twelve years.

Purchase of the *Puccini nelle imagine,* on which the guardian affixes — as a souvenir — the museum seal.

What comes out of this album:

Puccini and his taste for modern machines (cars, motor canoe, pleasure boat, radio, etc.) like Butterfly and her telescope (when she gazes at the gunboat *Lincoln* moored in Nagasaki bay): an "exotic" marveling at the progress of mechanical civilization;*

physical, et temporal, relationship between Puccini and Feydeau, Proust, Roussel, etc.

* Relationship with Futurism.

PUCCINI AND SCHOENBERG

"One must keep everything to oneself except the knowledge of things (*Sachverständnis*). What is this knowledge that we do not show?

I suppose it was the 'connoisseurs' who received my *Pierrot lunaire* in so unfriendly a way when I conducted it in Italy, and not the friends of art (*Kunstfreunde*). I had the honor of meeting Puccini, who is not a 'connoisseur' (*Sachverständiger*) but a producer (*Sachkönner*) (and) who, although already ill, traveled for six hours to hear my work. Afterwards, he made some friendly comments to me. It was beautiful, even if my music remained foreign to him." (Arnold Schoenberg, "Mein Publikum," *Der Querschnitt,* April 1930, p 223).

Account of the meeting by an eyewitness: Guido Marotti, "Incontri e colloqui col Maestro" (in *L'Approdo musicale,* 2nd year, no. 6, April–June 1959, ERI, Turin). From this account, we learn that Puccini had indeed been very curious about the new music but that he hadn't at all enjoyed listening to it. Perhaps he would have demonstrated the same kind of curiousity about the latest automobile?

DISCOVERY OF MONTEVERDI

When Paul Eluard's body lay in state the day before his funeral, a recordplayer played passages from *Orfeo,* a work that Eluard was particularly fond of (which is why his wife Dominique had chosen this music, as she told me some time after the ceremony). I don't believe I had ever heard anything by Monteverdi before that. What recordings did Dominique play? I have no idea, and all I can say is that I found the music beautiful, nothing more.

In September 1959, I attended an entire Monteverdi festival in Venice: a performance of *Orpheus* and of *The Fight between Tancredi and Clorinda,* recitals of *Arianna's Lament* (one version for soprano and another for vocal ensemble), *Vespers for the Virgin Mary,* madrigals, etc.

Before these Italian productions, I didn't realize how vehement this music was. With its highly "expressionistic" character, it prefigured great operatic art, which reached its high point with Puccini.

Astonishing vocal modulations, with breathtaking changes in rhythm and dynamics.

The *Orpheus,* so much more moving and beautiful than Glück's, and in no way emasculated by a "happy ending." Exquisiteness of the "pastoral" sections.

Similar to both Gongora and *Penthesilea* of *Tracredi and Clorinda.*

The Mexican Oralia Dominguez (soloist in *Tancredi* and mezzo-soprano in the *Vespers*), when she sings Monteverdi, gives the impression of *cante jondo.*

The bass aria (Seneca?) of the *Coronation of Poppaea,* already very "Phillipe II's aria."

In the *Vespers,* the choral passages are so rich, you think you're hearing a real live crowd.

It was in Monteverdi's work that René Char found his title *Lettera amorosa.*

A combination of violence and the most extreme delicacy, not unlike the best Racine. The pantomime in *Tancredi and Clorinda,* as it was given in the courtyard of the Cà Peraro, was unforgettable: the physical combat which reminds one of very physical lovemaking; Tancredi taking the blood of the wounded Clorinda in his hand to drink it, then taking water in his helmet to baptize her before the cross formed by the hilt of his sword.

Tancredi and Clorinda: the entire opera given in less than an hour, with three soloists, two dancers and a small orchestra.

Monteverdi's great inventions:

the "tremolo" (inspired by Plato, according to whom fast modes are appropriate for expressing intense emotions);

the opera house which charges for admission (in Venice in 1637 and *sqq.,* he created public opera houses, which were active during carnival season; he staged works by Manelli and Ferrari, as well as his own dramatic works, among them *L'Incoronazione di Poppea*).

THE MARRIAGE OF THETIS AND PELEUS

In 1959, I saw the nautical staging of this opera (on rafts and pontoons) which took place in the ornamental lake on San Giorgio island in Venice.

An incredible mess. Unable to get to their numbered seats (that others had taken), many spectators had to sit on the ground.

The terror of certain singers when, tangled up in their Greek costumes and buskins, they had to clamber over small boats which took them to the raft or pontoon that made up the stage.

Great cold, stiff segments alternating with scenes in comic opera style. But never, whether he was serious or light-hearted, did Cavalli manage to attain Monteverdi's marvelous intensity.

LA NINFA FIDELA[6]

Seeing this beautiful but hardly exciting opera by
Vivaldi, one would hardly suppose that – with *The
[Four] Seasons,* for example – he was one of the
first to compose what today we call "program
music." Performance style: the singing, like the
costumes, too flashy?

JEPHTA

Renneut and Neher's (Brecht's set designer) production for this oratorio by Handel, as staged by the Stuttgart Opera.

No sets but a perfectly symmetrical scenic device with a back wall in the form of a semicircle. The choruses and soloists (except for the prophet who, in the end, plays the role of the *deus ex machina*) are constantly on stage: the chorus (the most distant of whom, placed in a half-circle against the back wall, stand at times to sing but never *act*) facing the public; the soloists (three men on the left, two women on the right) sitting on stools with their backs turned.

The closest chorus members and soloists never sing without *acting,* generally on the podium that occupies the center of the stage.

Music in action rather than a performed opera, the movements of the characters are always in rhythm and stylized. {Very harsh criticism from Marcel Moré, who was with us on Monday 10/

12/59 for the second of the performances given at the Paris Opera: "As if Isadora Duncan were dancing to a Beethoven symphony…"}

The importance of props: severed heads stuck on lances for the opening Pagan dance, signs (most of them in the form of trophys with helmets and breastplates) of the departure for war, etc. The very *concrete* – and, for this reason, moving – character of these props.

Heights reached with half-glimpsed scenes – transparent thanks to the lighting effects – behind the semicircular back wall: the departure for war (half-silhouettes rendered by the reflections of helmets and breastplates), occuring from left to right and the return of the defeated – from right to left – to illustrate the dream of Jephta's wife; at the moment of the real departure for war, we get a glimpse of the Ark of the Covenant, half-covered by a piece of dark red cloth. Here, the very *spirit* of the music is achieved, for you only half-see and guess; things are not shown in black and white, but are only evoked. This red, these metallic reflections are not unlike that which, literarily, I would like to suggest between the lines: "Weber's stifled sighs" that Baudelaire spoke of (taking the opposite approach of Neher since, in the quatrain of *Phares,* he creates a music for Delacroix[7]).

The props – generally of a more "Roman" than "Jewish" character – play up the Baroque pomp of Handel's music. The work's religious aspect is marked in a permanent way by the costumes of the chorus members and by that of Jephta's daughter, clothes that are all somewhat sacerdotal.

In the flies, a very large circle (a little like the coping of an enormous inverse well): the expression of the cosmic and the divine.

IL MONDO DELLA LUNA

This ravishing comic opera – absolutely on Hadyn's level from a musical point of view – never really comes off dramatically.

As it was staged for the 1959 Holland Festival (and later given at Aix) it may have been crushed, more than supported, by its excessive production?

I recall feeling something similar a few years ago in Venice with Galuppi's *La Dianoluzza,* that they killed trying above all to fill it out.

DON GIOVANNI

A bearded Don Juan in 16th century dress inevitably brings Blue Beard to mind. When the Statue of the Commander intervenes, we witness the justifiable punishment of a hardy man whose excessive appetites have lead him to go too far, even with respect to God's condemnation of this Mephisto-like figure. In a stroke of genius, Cassandre set *Don Giovanni,* as it was given in Aix-en-Provence, in the era of Mozart and Da Ponte themselves, that is, in the 18th century: thus Don Juan is presented as a rake, a character who seems to have stepped out of the pages of the Marquis de Sade and who, when he confronts the Statue, is indeed the libertine of modern times at odds with the fearful defender of ideas from another age.

The first two years that *Don Giovanni* was produced at the Aix-en-Provence festival, Don Juan was played by an inimitable performer: Renato Capecchi, who was then all but a debutant.

Thin, youthful, alert, Capecchi, with his impertinence, knew how to use his lorgnette to ogle women's breasts (thus bringing out the central element of the drama: eroticism, which is almost always relegated to the background by performers undoubtedly afraid of appearing vulgar while trying to be gallant). This frail character knew how to welcome the Statue without flinching, torch in hand, his body extremely tense, and – after the fatal handshake and the repeated refusal to repent – plunge into the abyss with a long scream, writhing like a flame, his two arms raised desperately. Also noteworthy: the torero move to hide behind the red cape and thus avoid being recognized by Doña Anna (scene II, first act), and the way of singing the cavatina, very quickly, standing before the prompt box, legs spread and chest extremely rigid, his lower body blocked by the switch held in both hands.

Aren't the musical quotations in the last act (the "military aria" from the *Marriage,* etc.) – more than a game in the tradition of pure romantinc irony – a means of showing that time is now abolished, like at the moment of the Last Judgement? (It is unfortunate that we lose this anachronism with the 18th century production).

What I have never seen in a performer of Don Juan: his gargantuan eating and drinking at his last meal. Leporello is astonished and frightened by this gluttony – yet another offense against human and heavenly law. If Don Juan's excessive appetite for food isn't shown, as are his excessive eroticism and impertinence, the character is not complete.

DIE ZAUBERFLÖTE

The influence of 18th century ideas regarding ethnography and the history of civilizations perceptible in Mozart's *Magic Flute*: the initial prestige of Eastern Antiquity (Sarastro = Zoroaster, here a wise man of ancient Egypt), Papageno (a feathered man) and the "good savage," Monostatos the terrible African "Moor." Moreover, Tamino – who is not only a candidate for initiation, but is predestined – is a prince, as befits the era when freemasons recruited their members from among princes and their entourage.

The belief in racial hierarchy, implicit in the libretto: whites, feathered savages (Papageno and Papagena, who lack "religion," but are good, prolific, people), Blacks (Monostatos with his brutal appetites, being hand in glove with the Queen of the Night, that is, with man's dark side). What we have here is an non-concerted content superposed onto an intentional symbolism.

In all of opera, few things move me as much as, in *The Magic Flute,* the scene of the trial by fire and water that Tamino (armed with a magic instrument) and Pamina undergo, watched over by the two guardians of the threshold.

A scene that makes me cry (like a melody from a music box): Monostatos and his henchmen dancing to the sound of the glockenspiel shaken by Papageno.

I note that, in both of these scenes, music intervenes as such and is endowed with the highest powers, hence perhaps the emotion it provokes.

On June 7, 1942 I saw for the first time a performance of *The Magic Flute* at the Paris Opera. It was a matinée and there was a "gray mouse" in the balcony box where we sat. That was when Jews had to wear the yellow star. Walking home from the theater, I blushed with shame as I crossed a young Jewish couple on the Rue de Rivoli. Young and beautiful, they were both wearing stars, and stared passersby in the face as they walked by, hand in hand... (Like Tamino and Pamina braving the trial by fire and water.)

Imagine what a Wagnerian *Magic Flute* might be like, with Sarastro reciting the "Golden Verses" of Pythagoras!

To cut short this discussion, could the marvelous ever be a windbag?

Musically respected, this opera passes for being so dramatically weak that Wieland Wagner felt the need to call for a narrator (which permitted him to suppress the spoken scenes) and reduce the set to a minimum to give the whole work an oratorio feel.

Now, well sung and well directed (as it was by Knappertsbusch in May 1960 at the Paris Opera), *Fidelio* turns out to be a very moving drama which, even with a mediocre production, generates immediate enthusiasm: chronologically it is the first of the great Romantic operas.

The foolish fear of ridicule that leads people to emasculate the great works of the repertory simply because they do not dare perform them according to the rules of the game...

The aria of the *deus ex machina* Minister prefigures the Hermit's aria in the *Freischütz*.

The central role of the Prisoners' chorus.

MEDEA

Like Spontini's *Vestal Virgin,* Cherubini's *Medea* seems to link Glückian opera and Italian Romantic opera.

Beautifully solemn and serious arias. At times —during Medea's quarrel with Jason, for example — the tempo reaches a feverish pitch and you get caught up in the rhythm of a heart beating faster and faster, or a steam engine whose pistons must ever yield to a pressure that seems to intensify with each blow, in this supreme movement – simultaneously human and mechanical – that Bellini, Donizetti and Verdi can also create, but cannot better.

NORMA

I know *Norma* through the very beautiful recording that Callas made under the direction of Tullio Serafin, and through an Italian performance at the Enghien Casino, a performance that wouldn't have been bad if the role of Norma had been appropriately played…

In 1957, I heard "Casta diva" sung on the Piazza della Repubblica in Florence, in a café where we often went to hear the baritone and soprano who would alternate opera arias and light songs belted out by another pair of singers who represented the radio or music hall style.

According to Giulini, if Bellini's music is so difficult to sing, it is not so much because it requires great maturity, but rather because of its extraordinary purity, which so few performers can attain.

In 1964, Maria Callas sang *Norma* at the Paris Opera. A tremendous success dramatically, but deserving of much criticism musically: not only were there wrong notes in the high register (which must have really been wrong for me to notice them), but the famous "Casta diva…" was entirely sidestepped (sung in a way that might be called "confidential," it was robbed of all its lyric fullness). That said, it was fascinating to watch the soprano carry on a triple battle: the battle – a theatrical one – of Norma, the battle of the singer of diminished means to overcome the music, and that of the woman and artist to conquer the public.

THE BARBER OF SEVILLE

How mysterious, this mystery that so insistently charges Rossini's music – whether dazzling or frankly comic – and this, in spite of the fact that he was (by all appearances) a *bon vivant*. For lack of a better explanation, we can talk of "genius" in such cases: like a man possessed, the man of genius is the bearer of something which transcends him.

The pure *lust for life,** expressed (as in Mozart or Offenbach) without pathos and outside of any religiosity, is perhaps what gives this music its strange resonance and makes it so moving, even in its gaity. Compare *Carmen,* the Viennese waltzes, the *paso doble,* etc. Also see Verdi's *Falstaff* and Chabrier's comic operas. However, it seems to me that, of them all, Rossini is the "strangest" (and,

---

* Is it not this same "lust for life" that so moves me in painters like Manet, Toulouse-Lautrec or, today, Bacon; and in poets like Apollinaire and Limbour?

conversely, Chabrier the closest to jubilation without necessarily intending to be so).

Would musical analysis permit us to define the strangeness that I perceive here? Or would this strangeness elude analysis, like the poetry in a given text or the beauty in a painting?

In Venice in September 1959, I saw at the Teatro Ridotto (a charming 18th century concert hall located on the same street as Harry's Bar) Paisiello's *Barber of Seville,* sung by the students of the conservatory, who had already been somewhat broken in. The division into scenes is more or less the same in Paisiello as in Rossini, and there is notably a "Figaro Aria" and a "Slander Aria." These two arias — which are in fact good in Paisiello — give the curious impression of being unsuccessful, for you can't hear them without thinking of Rossini's.

LUCIA DI LAMMERMOOR

Seeing or hearing *Lucia di Lammermoor,* I had never thought that Donizetti's opera – which is still very close to Bellini and full of *bel canto* – could, through Walter Scott, evoke the *roman noir* and, even without these intermediaries, arrive purely and simply at Shakespeare's poetry.

The performances given at the Paris Opera* with soprano Joan Sutherland and (I believe) the Covent Garden sets, were imbued with this Romanticism. Performed in such a way, and in such a context, the famous madness scene, with its perilous aria, evokes that of Lady Macbeth's delirium. We recognize Shakespeare, who set so many of his plays in Italy, in Donizetti's Italianism... Surely there was but one *English* soprano capable of that! It is true that J[oan] S[utherland] is Australian (and is thus Melba's fellow countrywoman) and not

* The 25th and 29th of April 1960, with costumes and production by Franco Zeffirelli.

English, so maybe there was but one Englishwoman – all right, not a dyed-in-the-wool Englishwoman – who could achieve a successful amalgam.

Unlike other composers who have written scenes of madness (Bellini, for example), did Donizetti forsee his own destiny when he wrote Lucia's folly?

Dramatic value of the singing: here the cries of a frightened bird (as they are stalagtites in the Queen of the Night's aria).

{Zeffirelli's treatment of the madness scene:}
No more headdress or wedding veil. Hair undone and white dress spattered with blood, Lucia – "the *bride* of Lammermoor" – appears at the top of a curved staircase, faltering, her hand tightly grasping a heavy, blood-covered dagger...

The first Verist opera: a "slice of life" performed in contemporary costume. The radical difference between a work like *La Traviata* and a work like the *Nozze di Figaro* (also performed in costumes from the author's period) is not only that the *Marriage* is set in a conventional Spain, but also that the plot in no way attempts to be a "slice of life."

It took a Romantic like Verdi to invent the Verist opera, just as it took Hugo the Romantic to write *Les Misérables,* Flaubert the Romantic to invent Naturalism. The Verist work as a particular type of historical reconstruction the Romantics were fond of: is the "slice of life" anything more than a slice of contemporary history?

The sociological and folkloric side of *La Traviata*: the myth of the big city (cf. Roger Caillois), the high society, Parisian wedding, the procession of the Bœuf Gras.

The consideration that this opera enjoys in the People's Republic of China, where it can be seen

97

as a critique of the relationship between the sexes in bourgeois society: caste prejudice toward the prostitute, who is used by the society that despises her.

Visconti's production for *La Traviata* at La Scala in Milan:

Lila de Nobili's sets evoke Manet's paintings;

at the party in the third act, the fortune tellers are women disguised as fairies, with masks and pointed, silver lamé hats; the entrance of the toreros is an entrance of gentlemen in tails, disguised with whatever is available (paper *monteras,* red masks, homemade red belts created by rolling pieces of material around their waists); one of them (played by a ballet dancer) dances a Spanish, *zapateado*-like dance as if he didn't know how to, but nevertheless pulls it off with a certain brilliance;

in the last act, Violetta's apartment is shown as she prepares to move (a step ladder for removing curtains, trunks, etc.);

when Violetta wants to go out with Alfredo, she puts on a hat with a ribbon, but she feels faint and the hat, having fallen backward yet hanging from her neck by the ribbon, flaps ridiculously against her back.

(How this production emphasizes both the work's Verism and the Verdian fantastic, with its ravishing, yet odd-looking, imitation fairies.)

Originally, *La Traviata* was (apparently) given in 18th century costumes, as it seemed impossible to have the work sung in modern dress. In the Museum at La Scala in Milan, a copy of the reduction for piano and voice is shown (Ricordi, publisher):

the engraving on the cover shows Violetta and Alfredo in 18th century dress.

The libretto of *La Traviata*: a long party, interrupted by an interlude in the countryside and concluded with a collapse into ruin and death (with carnival sounds from the wings).

IL TROVATORE

Il Trovatore is generally regarded as the classic example of an opera with an extravagant libretto which, moreover, doesn't really count, since only the vocal performances are important. Yet it seems that, if you take *Il Trovatore* for what it is – a lyric drama whose extreme Romanticism is indicative of the "frenetic" type – you could stage it in such a way that the music would be more appropriate and the action convincing. Is the story of two enemy brothers, who only know they are enemies, not brothers, any more absurd than, for example, that of *Ruy Blas* replacing Don César de Bazan? Are the moments of bravura any more out of place in this story than the great tirades of Hugo's plays?

As for the sets and costumes, the Gypsy camp should make you think of a painting by Magnasco: darkness in which weapons, helmets and breastplates gleam, and out of which emerge disturbing figures in rags, some of them lame. The convent should evoke a Middle Ages out of Célestin

Nanteuil or Gustave Doré, and the fortified town, even the prison should seem Piranese-like.

As for the performers, their physiques should be in harmony with the unseen side of the action. The two brothers, Manrico and the Count di Luna, should resemble one another like Menaech-muses,[8] with the difference that the former has the tanned skin of a man who spends his life on the roads, with tousled hair and dressed like a truck driver, while the second, in his own get-up, has the aristocratic pallor of those who spend their lives in dimly-lit castles. The Gypsy Azucena, rather than an old hag or slut, should be an ageless woman, beautiful rather than ugly, a phantom or reincarnation of her mother who burned at the stake. In all of her attitudes, gestures, movements, Leonora should be harmonious and elegiac (more or less as the American Margherita Roberti played her in Paris in 1958 at the Théatre des Champs-Elysées).

As for the production, it should be resolutely picturesque: very turbulent battles, both individual and collective, as in Shakespeare when played by the English; particular attention should be paid to the way in which the Gypsies are presented at the forge (shown either making or repairing weapons) so that the hammer blows on the anvils produce a titillating – but not laughable – effect; nuns either frightened or already prepared for martyrdom; etc.

One of the first jazz compositions was an adaptation of the "Miserere" from *Il Trovatore* (cf. Alan Loman, *Mister Jelly Roll*[9]).

Frequent parodies of *Il Trovatore*: the Marx Brothers' film *A Night at the Opera*; the "Miserere" in the Crazy Gang Review in London.

A MODEL OPERA:
UN BALLO IN MASCHERA[10]

Just as there is occasionally "a play within a play" (cf. the scene with the actors in *Hamlet*), in its final tableau, Verdi's work offers us an "opera within an opera": a party (which is what traditional opera is, and which we find in many a modern opera, *Wozzeck* and *Peter Grimes,* for example, with their cabaret scenes) and, what's more, a mascarade (which is what any kind of theatrical performance is).

The page – a woman's role – as a transvestite ringleader of the tragic game: he's the one who leads the governor and his friends to the evil diviner, and who, in the last act, innocently denounces the disguised governor to the murderers.

The function of the game: it's fate that, through the cards, designates the one who is to kill the governor.

Leitmotiv of the laugh (a laugh integrated in the music: the governor's aria, when he laughs at the prediction, the conspirators' duo in the act in the cemetery).

Music from the grave (prelude to the ball).

Dramatic themes of foreboding:

the crowd of messengers of peace (transvestites portraying very young people) → flower-girls;

Rienzi and his sister → tetralogical (and other) acts of incest;

burning of the Capitol → destruction of Walhalla;

musically, Rienzi's prayer and the end of Tristan?

Heard in Leipzig, June 30, 1966, in a production reminiscent of Brecht (cf. *Coriolanus*).

Among the Bellinian echoes: Adriano Colonna, the tragic role of the transvestite mezzo, like Romeo of the [*I Capuletti e i Motecchi*].

Dramatic and musical exuberance of this play in which W[agner] apparently wanted to put everything.

As in *La Muette de Portici,* it seems, and as (later)

in *Boris Godounov,* the main role returns to the people: Wagner's Bakuninian era.

Great theatrical effects, as in the historical operas of Meyerbeer and Verdi: unsheathed swords, processional crosses and banners, the "lightning" of excommunication, flames from the stake…

The work is labeled: "Great Tragic Opera," while *The Flying Dutchman* will be a "Romantic Opera."

Political plot (the man of the people against the aristocrats, then against the clergy) with a secondary, "passionate" plot (the young aristocrat and the tribune's sister).

TRISTAN UND ISOLDE

9/3/66 — It is announced that a *Tristan and Isolde,*
directed by Pierre Boulez and staged by Wieland
Wagner, will be given in Osaka (Japan). The Noh
or, more generally, Japanese theater aspects of
Tristan: the rarely broken immobility of the characters, King Mark and his long modulated monologue, the feudal ethic (cf. the Samurai and their
Overlord), the double death of the lovers (cf. the
double suicides of Japanese theater). In this particular case, Wieland Wagner's excessively stripped
down style could be marvelous.

(The musical declamation of Japanese and Chinese actors, Wagnerian speeches, modern
"Sprechgesang.")

DIE MEISTERSINGER

A monument erected by Wagner to the glory of lyric inspiration and before whom I'm probably quite wrong to act disgusted.

A musically admirable, ideologically irreproachable* movement whose sole fault is undoubtedly that it is a little too "monumental."

The painful side: the titan Richard Wagner trying his hand at good-natured comedy, though he lacks the casualness and verve of a Victor Hugo.

---

* However, some one recently pointed out to me that the libretto of the *Meistersinger* contains attacks on the "Welsch" (i.e. the French) which reveal a highly unpleasant chauvinism (7/4/78).

PARSIFAL

Personal memories of *Parsifal*: 1914, I was led into a box just off stage, and was so proud to be taken to see a work that was reputed to be "difficult" that I didn't even think about being bored; at the time of my affair with D.S.,[11] I went to meet her in Wiesbaden on the pretext of seeing *Parsifal,* but I couldn't get a seat and that – together with my disorientation and depression at being in occupied territory – moved me to return to Paris the day (or two days?) after my arrival; finally, March 26, 1954, I saw *Parsifal* given in Paris, by the Stuttgart Opera.

Isn't the second act – with Klingsor's incantation and the tableau of girl-flowers – the most attractive musically, which would mean that William Blake was right in his aphorism on Milton, more at ease in *Paradise Lost* than in *Paradise Regained* because "the poet is always on the side of the demons without knowing it"?

Isn't wanting to exclude the "bravos" (as they are contrary to religious reverence), in fact, a desire to suppress the intervention of the public and, reducing it to passivity, hinder all real communication between the performers and it (communication by definition cannot be unilateral), which amounts to depriving the theatrical event of its truly "ritual" component: this suddenly manifested communion?

{On the ideological contents of *Parsifal,* cf. [*supra*] "'Committed' Operas." On *Parsifal* as a rite, cf. [*supra*] "Wagner Librettist."}

LA BELLE HÉLÈNE

I would like to understand why I am not only over-joyed, but moved nearly to tears by this alternation of exquisite arias and *Farmers' Almanack*-like jokes. I am obviously sensitive to the myth of the *Belle Epoque*: nostalgic for the time of my childhood and before.

With Offenbach was there not a nostalgia – veiled by irony – for the Greek gods? {Cf. Leibowitz, *Histoire de l'opéra* [Paris: Buchet-Chastel, 1957]: "Nostalgia for a Lost Innocence"}.

In the first chapter of *Nana,* Zola describes a performance of *La Belle Hélène* or of *Orphée aux enfers*; for him, a sign of the corruption of the times.

The most boring of the various *Fausts*: Gounod's, which is trivial but pleasant; Boito's (*Mefistofele*), likable for its gigantic ambition (Italian opera reconciled with German opera, like, for Goethe, Classicism and Romanticism, Greek Antiquity and the Middle Ages); Busoni's, which is totally fantastic; and Berlioz' "grand machine," which is dull and without structure.*

The Paris Opera's pathetic attempt to bring new life to this opera (March 1964); the Maurice Béjart production, with its childish eroticism (instead of showing fake nude women – i.e. in skin-colored bodysuits – why not strip them *within acceptable limits*? That would be more effective erotically than a cleaned-up Folies Bergères). Furthermore, the overburdened production takes away from the music: an aria does not need to be illustrated by

---

* But perhaps its structure would be more apparent if we were to take the work for what it actually is: an oratorio.

the movements of a dancer circulating around the singer. A valid idea for the last scene: Faust's damned soul represented by a male dancer standing on his head, while Marguerite's saved soul is represented by a female dancer (in a white bodysuit, like her partner) whose silhouette, seen from behind, stands at the top of a staircase, her arms raised; this is surely simplistic symbolism, but it is rather successful as an "effect."

Everything has now been so distorted that various newspapers have actually credited – as if it were some sort of victory – the Nouvel Opéra (direction: Auric) with the fact that the new production of the *Damnation*...was booed by a fraction of the public: proof, not of the weak staging of the work, but rather of its "scandalous" character.

Whatever we might say in favor of Gounod, his vulgarity is clearly expressed in what he made of *Faust*: a little love story fringed with devilry — which neither Berlioz did with the *Damnation,* nor Boito with *Mefistofele,* nor Busoni with *Il Dottore Faust*.

The "church scene" that I sang as a child, doing my best to sing in a bass voice.

The most favorable idea that I've had of *Faust,* after hearing it at the Baths of Caracalla: the Mephisto character's comic side (notably in the "garden scene," with the alternating duos, Faust and Marguerite's being lyrical, the Devil and the duenna's comical), the famous soldiers' chorus, sung "in situation" (with a brillant parade, including — of course! — cavalrymen), a very lively kermesse, etc. A strange omission: the aria Mephisto sings to Marguerite as she prays in the church. On the other hand, an aria that I had never heard (or never heard well, as it was too poorly sung to pay attention to it): that of Valentine alone, after the soldiers' return. "Walpurgis Night" cut (I shall see and hear it one more time, staged separately as a ballet).

MIGNON

I had forgotten that the "dance of the eggs" was a scene from *Mignon*. My older sister told me the story long ago, and I feared for the kidnapped girl who had to accomplish her difficult task without making a mistake, or be beaten and whipped.

At the Musée Rodin, two busts (at least one in bronze) representing "Mignon."

Ambroise Thomas, who wrote *Mignon* on a libretto taken from the *Wilhelm Meister's Journeyman Years,* also authored a *Hamlet.** Now, in Goethe's novel the protagonist stages Shakespeare's *Hamlet*. Perhaps this is not a coincidence?

---

* First performed by the baritone [Jean-Baptiste] Faure, of whom Manet painted a portrait in this role and of whom Verdi wrote, in a letter of 1882, that of all the singers of the Paris Opera, he alone was not "very mediocre." When I was a child, this opera was my favorite, undoubtedly because of its libretto (simulated madness).

MEFISTOFELE

Arrigo Boito was determined to put everything in it: both of Goethe's *Fausts*, and both Verdi's and Wagner's music. The ambition of this man – who was, for Verdi, a skillful, modest librettist – is so overblown here that it leaves one confused and unable to judge the work.

Mefistofele at the San Carlo in Naples*: the bass Nicola Rossi-Lemeni (Mefistofele) appears behind a screen of clouds, singing a grand aria for the Prologue in Heaven; the "Walpurgis Night," with Mefistofele wearing a huge, transparent ball which is the sphere of the world, with also multiple *entrées de ballet,* one of which is a skeletons' dance; Mefistofele and Faust in medieval dress among the ballerinas wearing Greek tunics and Queen Helen of Sparta herself; and the final temptation of Faust,

* On a Sunday afternoon, a staging at "extremely popular" prices.

behind whom, as the background gradually becomes transparent, Mefistofele parades a series of half-naked women in lascivious poses who will be replaced — when Faust triumphs — by a (no less suggestive) group of women dressed as angels and bearing long trumpets, posing like the sculptures that adorn baroque churches.

I PAGLIACCI

Pagliaccio = a translation into Verist language of the most Romantic of themes: the impossibility of believing appearances (tears behind laughter, reality behind theater).

Having these two themes – tears behind laughter and truth behind theater – converge in a single work, Leoncavallo has perhaps made a discovery as great as that of Tirso de Molina when in the *Burlador de Sevilla,* he brought together the following two popular themes which until then had been distinct: the punished libertine, the murderous statue.

The two themes in question might seem, at first sight, opposed to one another: 1) what happens in the theater happens in reality (just as the play that Hamlet stages is true, as is King Claudius's distress on seeing it, which gives Hamlet proof that the specter told the truth, that it was indeed his father's ghost and not a spirit from hell); 2) flaunted gaity and comedy are but appearances (*The Man*

Who Laughs, the unhappy harlot/Fantine, Marguerite Gautier/Violetta, Manon, Mimi the consumptive grisette, the geisha Cio-Cio-San, the sad clown/Yorick the skull, Triboulet/Rigoletto). In 1) appearance is deemed truth; in 2) it is the exact opposite of truth. However, if you think about it, you see that the two themes coincide: in both cases, it is a question of showing that there is something serious behind a playful appearance.

Leoncavallo's stroke of genius, which procedes as if from the moment that all depends on the opposition of appearance and truth, it were indispensible – for the machine to function – that a truthful framework be strongly affirmed, which is just what "Verism" tends toward, with its excess realism.

You could say that something essential is at stake in any work whose success is understood by practically the entire western world (and such is the case for *I Pagliacci*), and that it is to a certain degree ingenious.

Exegesis: it has been said that Leoncavallo's libretto for *I Pagliacci* was inspired by a trivial event that occured in his home town (Naples) or in Calabria during his youth; it has also been said that he took the subject from *La Femme de Tabarin* by Catulle Mendès.

The "inside information," the wings: the author coming on stage at the end of Crabbe's *Sileni*; besides *I Pagliacci,* Leoncavallo's *Zazà* (which takes place in the wings of a *café-concert* and in the box of a "chanteuse"); Pirandello; Tzara's *Mouchoir de nuages.*

ARIADNE AUF NAXOS

The estheticism of this opera, with its deliberate blend (for no other reason than to be pretty) of the tragic and *commedia dell'arte* styles. It's not the composite character that irks, it's the intent: the piquant — and frankly esthete — strategy to which it responds. Compare it with another work, every bit as composite, *Un ballo in maschera*: in Verdi's work the different styles are justified by the nature of the characters and situations; in Richard Strauss' work, Hofmannsthal's libretto is imagined — and how poorly! — to justify the juxtaposition of the two styles.

> *Ariane, ma sœur, de quel amour blessée*
> *Vous mourûtes aux bords où vous fûtes laissée...*[12]

> [*Ariane, my sister, from what love wound*
> *Did you die on the shores where you were left behind...*]

Naxos: I visited the island in 1939. We stayed in a hotel whose owner answered to the name of "Nionios" (dimunitive of "Dionysus"). In the room, there was a little coil made of a light green substance that we burned at night to keep the mosquitoes away. That was the hotel in which Z[ette] (then at odds with me) forgot her belt. Passing through Naxos again on the way back from Santorin — just before the war — we saw Nionios approaching the boat, carrying the forgotten belt and explaining that he had boarded all the other boats in the hope of finding us.

THE WOMAN WITHOUT A SHADOW

With *The Woman without a Shadow,* Richard Strauss wrote his "triumph of love," as Puccini did with *Turandot.*

The deployment of all scenic and musical means that opera has to offer: transformation scenes, voices from the wings (especially "voices from above"), arias, duos, ensembles of several voices, choruses, etc. And the "marvelous" as if it were the very essence of opera, its form *par excellence* being in this case the following: the presence of an evil spell which, when broken, will bring about the final flowering of an intoxicating duo (*Turandot*) or double duo (*The Woman without a Shadow*).

In the libretto Hofmannsthal wrote for *The Woman without a Shadow,* the "triumph of love" grows out of a triumph of procreation. There was also a "triumph of love" in Wagner's *Tristan and Isolde,* with the difference that the two lovers came together in death (a theme present in *Aïda* as in *Norma*), which does not deliver them from a spell, since it is – on the contrary – from a spell (the potion) that their love came about.

Another "triumph of love," *The Magic Flute*: the loving couple overcomes the ordeals of initiation and is finally brought together by the one who presides over their initiation.

PELLÉAS ET MÉLISANDE

Today it seems surprising that *Pelléas et Mélisande* was taken as a model to follow by the anti-Wagnerians. Though it might have brought something new to opera (the rejection – or at the very least, discrete use – of *leitmotive,* the omission of long passages of sung speech, cutting the action up into a series of brief tableaux linked by interludes, as Alban Berg would later do in *Wozzeck*), Claude Debussy's work does in fact remain very Wagnerian: the use of a legendary subject not unlike that of *Tristan,* the orchestra / voice relationship that justifies the reproach made to Wagner of having placed the statue in the orchestra pit and the pedestal on the stage, the musical influence of *Parsifal,* etc.

From a contemporary perspective, we can consider that *Pelléas et Mélisande* represented the end result of Wagnerism – and, if you like, its crowning achievement – rather than the opening of a truly new path in music. From the same perspective, it paradoxically seems that Puccini – scorned for so long by people of taste, at least in France – was a greater innovator in opera than Debussy. For though a "Verist," he is also an "Expressionist" and, by that very fact, prefigures a few of the most beautiful modern operas.

Could Debussy have penned one of those masterpieces which (as it often happens) differ greatly from the one the author intended to write, but which are nevertheless masterpieces? It's impossible not to think of Baudelaire writing *Le Spleen de Paris,* and Roussel writing his novels, the former thinking of Aloysius Bertrand, and the latter, Jules Verne and, far from attempting to do the opposite, nevertheless strayed in spite of themselves from their models. You'd wish that Debussy, following the example of these two indisputable innovators, were both less Wagnerian and more Wagneristic, and that, contrary to what he intended, he had done something entirely different from his glorious predecessor.

LOUISE

The musical use of the "cries of Paris."

The Verist libretto (supposedly penned by Saint-Pol Roux).

In his *Lenin* (the chapter "Lenin and the Former *Iskra*"), Trotsky relates how, when Vladimir Ilich came to Paris to give three lectures on the agrarian question at the Ecole des Hautes Etudes Sociales, "we decided to take him to the opera. N.I. Sedova, a member of the *Iskra*, was to take him there. Vladimir Ilich went to the Opéra-Comique and came back with the satchel which never left his side when he went to give his lecture at the Ecole des Hautes Etudes. The opera in question was *Louise*, by Gustave Charpentier, a work with a very democratic subject. There was a group of us on the upper circle. Besides Lenin, Sedova and myself, Martov was in attendance, if I recall. I do not remember who else might have been there with us. That visit to the Opéra-

Comique included a little incident which had nothing to do with the music but which left a strong impression on me. Lenin had bought a pair of shoes in Paris. They turned out to be too tight (…) As if by chance, I, too, needed new shoes. Lenin gave me his (…) I decided to wear them to the Opéra-Comique. They were fine on the way there, but in the theater, things began to go wrong. Maybe that's why I don't remember the impression the opera made on Lenin and me. I only know that he was more than inclined to make jokes and he laughed a great deal. On the way back, I was already suffering cruelly and Vladimir Ilich, entirely merciless, derided me the whole way home. There was however a certain commiseration in his scoffing: had he not himself endured the torture of these shoes for a few hours?"

In another chapter of the same work, "Truth and Lies about Lenin," Trotsky – criticizing the portrait that Gorky painted of Lenin – affirms that "in the person, in the face of Lenin, there is nothing that makes one think of an opera."

TOSCA

As Floria Tosca, Patricia Neway is so like one of those paintings by Boldini – now adorned with a Surrealist patina – that it is shocking to see her in front of a Mario Cavaradossi lacking a Salvador Dali-like antenna mustache.

Part of the *Tosca* folklore that every director should respect: the great coquette's long cane that she carries at her entrance in the first act with the bouquet of flowers, a pious offering to the Madonna; the crucifix that she places around the neck of the stabbed Scarpia at the end of the second act. On the pretext of "dusting off" masterpieces, they wind up mutilating them. The *tour de force* accomplished by André Barsacq in his new presentation of *Tosca* for the Paris Opera (June 1960): he turns it into something cold and boring for fear of falling into melodrama – not unlike wanting to stage *Ruy Blas* in the same style as *Le Cid*. The parallel *tour de force* accomplished by the conductor

(Georges Prêtre) who, having his musicians play consistently too loud, abolishes all dramatic progression and, in addition, often hampers his singers.

MADAME BUTTERFLY

Before the First World War, my parents took me to the Opéra-Comique to see Marguerite Carré in *Madame Butterfly,* a role she played in the style of a great tragic actress. She sang terribly, and an Englishman who was sitting near us struck the balcony railing with a tuning fork, as if he didn't dare believe his ears and was determined to check — then left in disgust.

<In Amsterdam's Red Light district, there is a "Butterfly Concert" next door to a "Café Traviata.">
The fox-trot *Poor Butterfly.*
{Cf. *[infra]* "Maria Meneghini Callas" and "Operas on Film"}

The extreme taste that the performance and staging of this opera demands, though it all too often falls into unbearable Japanese kitsch.

TURANDOT

In July 1947, Constant Lambert had directed it, unsuccessfully, in Covent Garden. That's when I met Constant Lambert: at a party given by Isabel Delmer and her friend Anna Philips — at whose house she was living. Constant Lambert arrived quite late, wearing his black conductor's suit, a button missing from his shirt front; horribly drunk, and very much in love with Isabel (whom he married shortly after). Isabel Delmer, with whom I dined that evening, had proposed that we either stop by Covent Garden to see the end of the show, or that we go to a music hall, for at the time I thought (as I was supposed to) very little of Puccini, and on top of that had no desire to see only the end of an opera. That same evening, I believe, Anna Philips told me that *Turandot* was an astonishing ("sado-masochistic") work, insisting on the beauty of all those people "shouting at the same time."

In Rome a few years later, I saw a scene of

Turandot in the film of Giacomo Puccini's life. I then understood Anna Philips' insistence on the importance of the choral masses in this work.

Later still, at Louis Clayeux's place, I heard a good part of the recording made with Inge Borkh, Renata Tebaldi, Mario del Monaco, etc.

Finally, on September 13, 1958, I was given a recording of *Turandot,* directed by Serafin, in the Scala de Milan series. The extraordinary beauty of those moments when the chorus *shouts.* The Emperor of China in a very frail tenor voice (= the Innocent of *Boris Godounov* and the Mercanti of *La Forza del destino*), which not only expresses the character's old age, but seems to situate him at some fantastic distance.

Today, I am troubled more than ever by the *faux pas* I made in *L'Age d'homme* when I spoke badly of Puccini: aside from *Turandot,* I can't think of an opera in which the characters of Judith (Turandot) and Lucrecia (Liù) are on stage simultaneously. In *Tosca* you already had the woman who kills, and in *Madame Butterfly* the woman who kills herself.*

* p. 104, line 2: ...*that other piece of trash by Puccini.*

The "Expressionistic" character of the music in *Turandot,* and of Puccini's work in general. This expression is what makes *Turandot* a very 20th century work, no less so than *Wozzeck,* for example, or the *Dreigroschenoper.*

Turandot's symbolic system: through her voluntary death, Liù/Lucrecia offers Turandot/Judith one last victim, and lifts the evil spell that weighed on her as she strove to protect Calaf/Holofernes.

To the three fatal questions he triumphantly answered, Calaf adds a fourth. His question will

---

A long note to add here, indeed an appendix entitled *Amende à Giocomo Puccini* which is counterpart to *De la littérature [considérée comme une tauromachie].*

The discovery I made of the Italian Verist opera in *I Pagliacci* at the Rome Opera and *The Girl of the Golden West* at the San Carlo in Naples.

Verism = Naturalism, different from Naturalism à la Zola (because it's not symbolic) but like Naturalism à la Maupassant (because it's not photographic); Verism = in fact, Naturalism which only retains certain climactic elements of reality.

I long misunderstood Puccinian vehemence – the value of this vehemence – which makes him seem so "with it" today: vehemence which links him to the Richard Strauss of also prove to be fatal, as it brings about Liù's torture and suicide. In asking a question himself, Calaf sets in motion the mechanism that will ultimately disarm the woman who questioned him: having wagered his life on this additional riddle and having triumphed for the fourth time, he puts himself at the mercy of the woman he questioned, then he himself responds to his own question when he gives her his name. Having correctly answered the princess's three riddles, Calaf leads a sort of game of "the loser wins" in which he will conquer the princess by turning himself over to her.

Elektra and of *Salome,* yet also relates him to the Expressionists (cf. Alban Berg with Büchner's *Wozzeck* and Wedekind's *Lulu*).

Besides, the terrible, unexpected topicality of *Tosca*'s libretto: the torture and the firing squad;

L'Age d'homme is, in a way, a Verist book: basically, only climactic elements of reality have been retained.

What I am saying, in this book, about images representing news items also poses the question of Verism.

Verism as a means of going beyond art for art's sake: you are beyond art the moment that you become attached to such crises and, especially, when you provoke them. Through these crises you arrive at a living reality – like in bullfighting?

The story of Turandot and the prince as a story of courtly love: the inadequacy of the regular trials that the lover's complete, gratuitous sacrifice will complete.

Three deaths in the opera *Turandot*: the young Prince of Persia, the slave Liù and the composer himself. Fate decreed that Puccini would not survive the slave Liù. You might also say that everything happens as if, at the moment of the happy ending, he had to make way for Alfano.

Virgins who decapitate, slit throats or simply murder: Turandot, Salome, Elektra, Penthesilea, Marcel Schwob's perverse little girls...

Orléans, March 7, 1954

De Quincey's Verism in the murder accounts of *Murder as One of the Fine Arts,* indeed in the episode of Ann of the *Confessions.*

As a rule, Verism finds its inspiration in the social milieux that stand on the edges of society: the underworld; the world of prostitution or of theater, vagabonds, wretches, etc. Systematically seeking out in the present book everything that comes from "Verism" (children climbing trees barefoot, for example)... But the social theme sketched out on page 225 has nothing to do with Verism: it's much too "quotidian"![13]

137

We can imagine a *Turandot* by Mallarmé, instead of his *Hériodiade*. If — as it seems, according to Mallarmé — the artist or poet is a John the Baptist who must die in himself to give birth to beauty, this type of sacrifice is curiously illustrated by Puccini's fate, since he died while working on *Turandot,* a tragedy that has a Hérodiade as its main character. In this light, the fact that at the Torre del Lago villa, Puccini's remains lie practically in his piano takes on a highly symbolic character. That Puccini had thought nothing of all that and that he had only sought glory — vulgar glory — as a means of escaping time, that makes his fate all the more remarkable.

Certain people wish to be buried with an object they were particularly fond of (a portrait or sentimental souvenir, a jewel, professional instrument, etc.). Puccini has himself buried — or happens to be buried — in (or right next to) the object that perpetuated his memory and symbolized his work: his piano. Dead, he is but his work, he dissolves into it, is absorbed.

The invocation to the moon at the beginning of *Turandot*. The moon, a frigid goddess, Mallarmé, Laforgue. See the mythology of Diana.

Compare the tale of Psyche: here, the stranger says his name without any prompting, and afterward his lover baptizes him L O V E.

Calaf's *Igitur*-side: no throw of the dice, but the question / suicide.

Turandot= high tragedy (constantly alternating terror and pity) + Chinese Orientalism (both barbarian and refined) + Italian comedy (the three ministers). A successful synthesis, very different (and certainly more interesting) than the *Ariadne auf Naxos* undertaking, a deliberately composite work in which Richard Strauss juxtaposes and opposes *opera seria* and *opera buffa* on a disingenuous pretext in no way embellished by Hofmannsthal.

The simple, effective means used by Puccini who, from this point of view, can be considered "classical."

The "minute of silence" marking the moment that death forced Puccini to hand over the pen to Alfano should be adopted for *all* performances of *Turandot*: technically, it would show that Alfano is going to deal the final blow — without attempting to shine (as is only right) — to the bull that took out his predecessor: metaphysically, this would be the equivalent of the "blows struck in *Macbeth*" (a manifestation of fate, following De Quincey).

Turandot at la Scala (March 1960). Strokes of genius in the staging: the androgenous beings carrying hammers and nails preceding the Prince of Persia as he is lead away to be tortured (their graceful poses, their youth); the procession of decapitated suitors (sorts of ancient statues with huge, vague robes, carrying their heads in their right arms); after the prince strikes the gong three times, the gong opens up and through it the prince enters the pavillon at the top of which stands Turandot: a veritable descent into hell; at the end of the question scene, young girls – virginal flower in hand – swirling streamers in the air to cheer on the prince (which recalls certain details of the Chinese national holiday).

The Thousand and One Days (Persian tales whose Arabic original, *Al-Faradj b'ad alchidda* = the joy that comes after the pain, was translated into Turkish and is better known in this form) ➡ "fiabish" play by Gozzi (taken from a folktale, with serious, written parts and comic parts in *commedia dell'arte* style) ➡ Schiller's translation (for which C.M.Weber wrote incidental music) ➡ operas by Busoni and Puccini.

"This work, made up of tales strung one after another, shows us a princess warned against men, yet all the tales in this collection tend to undermine this warning" (*Nouveau Larousse illustré,* s.n. "Mille-et-un-jours").

Double "Chinese" style in the music of *Turandot*: an archaistic style (the barbaric tragedy of heavy choral or orchestral masses and soli such as the readings of the Mandarin, the Emperor's declaration, the questions and answers), an orientalist style (adoring or imploring choruses and, mixed with a *commedia dell'arte* style, everything about the three ministers).

Calaf triumphs through love (which allows him to escape death). But if Puccini also triumphs, it is not through love but through art — exactly: through *art for love's sake* (different from "art for art's sake").

Puccini's words, spoken during the composition of *Turandot*: "The opera will be given incomplete and someone will come on stage and say: 'At this point the *Maestro* died.'" (quoted by André Gauthier, *Puccini* [Paris: Seuil, 1961], 154).

While he was working on *Turandot* and already ill, Puccini traveled to Via Reggio in Florence to hear the first Italian performance of *Pierrot lunaire* by Arnold Schoenberg. A final voyage of curiosity and passionate, not unlike the one he had made at seventeen years of age (Lucques–Pisa round trip on foot, about 40 kilometers) to attend a performance of *Aïda*.

Woman, always a "femme fatale" (dangerous, perfidious, scheming, etc.) in the work of Gozzi, who still seems to fear her (cf. *Mémoires inutiles*).

An opera that isn't even a good copy of Puccini (as I thought it would be); it falls short. Listening to Giordano made me think of Ponchielli.

A few arias bring out the good qualities of the singers.

The theme of the "murdered poet" bogged down in (counter-revolutionary) imagery of the French Revolution. The sole (pataphysic) pleasure offered by this imagery is that everything is simultaneously present, creating an incredible hodge-podge: *sans culottes,* knitters, Republican soldiers, fops, coxcombs, the Revolutionary tribunal, victims from the nobility (including one nun), etc.

Historically, André Chénier — an irreligious, debauched man — was a libertine in full sense of that term. Mlle de Coigny (the *Jeune Captive* that the poet noticed in prison) was in fact a young woman of very easy morals: with the proper financing, she escaped death, as did her lover, who was also a prisoner. Under the Restoration, she became a highly respected *femme de lettres* who wrote chiefly to advocate what today we call "free love."

Unlike Puccini's *Manon Lescaut* (so close to the Abbé Prévost's heroine), Giordano's *Andrea Chénier* doesn't leave anything out, neither from the historical nor the legendary Chénier: a flat imitation of the letter scene in the last act of *Tosca,* that's all that's left of the famous episode of the *Iambes* written practically at the foot of the scaffold.

LULU

Thanks to Wedekind's libretto, we can see more clearly than in *Wozzeck* the extent to which Alban Berg is an "Expressionist" composer, as concerned with dramatic effect as a Puccini, for example.

The "Verist" character of this work, performed in contemporary (or nearly contemporary) dress, several scenes of which could have been taken from the newspapers (the sudden death of the husband, the murder of the lover, the escape, the meeting with Jack the Ripper).

The importance of the interludes, with respect to the atmosphere to be created.

In 1964, in Tokyo, I shall be thinking of *Lulu* and her tribulations on seeing a performance of a Verist play (the story of a beggar and a courtesan) at the Kabuki-za. This 19th century drama is the sequel to another play and thus has the "serialized" character of Wedekind's work, as he wrote two plays (fused into one by Alban Berg) on his heroine Lulu.

A musically rich work that thoroughly exploits the potential of combining *Sprechgesang* and singing.

A poor text (as in nearly all operas with a philosophical bias).

The Berlin Opera's absolutely appalling production (given in April 1961 at the Théâtre des Champs-Elysées): the stage designer wanted to be too modern and stupidly succeeded, revelling in needless complications. The acme of horror is reached with the orgy of the Golden Calf: the fake nude women in tights shaded with a bush of pubic hair (and zippers clearly visible on the back).

On the other hand, Covent Garden's very beautiful production (July 1965): staging by Peter Hall who, scrupulously following Schoenberg's directions, treats this opera not as an avant-garde work, but like any other opera. The highly successful scene of the Golden Calf: a little mule, goat and sheep, future sacrificial victims, parade across the stage; the blood flows like water; virtually naked,

Soho stripteasers play the immolated virgins; the sacrificers throw pieces of meat to the people, flinging them from one end of the stage to the other; at the moment of the orgy, people strip off their clothes and likewise fling them across the stage. The tremendous success of these productions: performed in this way, i.e. lacking any sophistication, Schoenberg's work doesn't seem to shock the uninitiated operagoer any more than another opera might!

THE THREE-PENNY OPERA

Returning from Africa in 1933, after a trip that lasted nearly two years, I had a hard time readapting to life in Paris. All of the shows I was taken to see seemed trivial, artificial and boring. The first one I was able to enjoy was *The Three-Penny Opera* (the French version of the film[14] — the German version I saw only later). That was (of course) because of the sententious allure of the songs and the hurdy-gurdy character of the music. Perhaps also because of the "Soho" or "mysteries of London" theme: the villains, criminals, prostitutes…, in a word, the furthermost reaches of *Fantomas* and Verism. The Hamburg-like quality of the bordello song. The Kipling-like quality of the song of the Indian army.

The common exquisiteness of the chanteuse Florelle, who never puts anything between parentheses.

A dream London, like that of *L'Emigrant de Landor Road*.[15]

Originally, the film *The Three-Penny Opera* seemed to be the work not of Pabst or Brecht, but rather that of composer Kurt Weill.

With *The Three-Penny Opera,* as with Brecht's other works that include songs (*Mother Courage,* for example), there is a renewal of the old "comic opera" genre, with alternating spoken and sung parts. There is also an analogy with Chinese theater, in which the crucial moments are sung.

The score of *The* [*Three-Penny*] *Opera* mustn't be taken (as it was when performed by Milan's Piccolo Teatro) for a parody of opera, cantatas, caf'conc'or music hall-style popular songs, etc. Rather, it brings into play a number of commonplaces borrowed from these various types of music, something like the music Satie spoke of, which would hold up even when poorly played, and by hack musicians. *The* [*Three-Penny*] *Opera* is undoubtedly a satirical work, but much more of a social satire than an esthetic satire (or parody). Thus, the use made of hackneyed esthetic forms is more the product of Romantic irony than of any antipoetic, derisive mode, which is what parody pure and simple actually is.

The words of Kurt Weill as reported by G.H. Rivière.[16] K[urt] W[eill] had just arrived in Paris, fleeing Nazism. In response to the attacks on his music, he declared: "I am an asphalt musician (i.e., a musician of the street)… But a German one!"

MAHAGONNY

The scaled-down version heard in 1934 (having heard the 1932 version) in the Salle Gaveau. Staging by Neher. Principal singer: Lotte Lenya; conductor: Maurice de Abravanel. The uncut version at the TNP, in November 1966. This latter version surprised me – and bowled me over with its non-ironic (through the simple use of formulas), extremely seductive and powerful, "grand opera"-like quality. The extraordinary power of the final choruses: "You can't help a corpse…" "No one can help anyone…" If a libretto has valid, literary qualities, you may as well translate it; I obviously wouldn't have felt such emotion hearing these choruses had I not understood the words.

The fact that this French performance – which was very good, unless you want to quibble – took place at the TNP makes one think that if opera is to be revived in France, it won't happen (barring a revolution) at the Théâtre national de l'Opéra. Rather, it will come from the periphery, and with marginal works like *Mahagonny* (that you can't really imagine in the context or before the public of old "Académie nationale de musique").

Less picturesque than *The Three-Penny Opera, Mahagonny* — as much on Weill's as on Brecht's part — certainly goes much further. Emphasized rather than covered up by the music, the extreme harshness of the libretto is perhaps the cause of this work's unpopularity.

Against the purists who demand that an opera be sung in the original language: it is a pity that a beautiful libretto (by Brecht or Büchner, for example) not be understood by the listeners. This purist demand amounts to the repudiation of all translations: no more Shakespeare in French, no more Calderón, no more Chekhov…

THE GAY DIVORCEE

A musical by Cole Porter that I saw in London in 1934, with Fred Astaire and Claire Luce. This is the work that features the famous tune "Night and Day," which was so beautifully staged in the film that was later made of it[17] (Fred Astaire standing about, waiting "night and day" in different types of clothes imposed by fashion for the various hours of the day: the informal suit worn in the morning, the proper suit with umbrella in the afternoon, "evening dress," etc., a sort of fashion plate parade unfolding in time to the song).

At that time, F[red] A[staire] knew how to move impassively from acting to dancing and song, then back to acting without giving you the impression he was just "doing a number," a talent he later lost or stopped taking advantage of.

Gershwin couldn't make up his mind: this work isn't really an opera, nor does it have the spontaneity of a Black variety show. Nevertheless, the Black performers pulled it off.

African-America folklore is represented in its entirety: work songs, spirituals, sermons, jazz, etc.

During the European tour of *Porgy and Bess,* I saw Gershwin's work at the Fenice in Venice, at the more or less gala première with (as usual) small bouquets of roses on the front of each of the boxes. The program is so vague that I can't figure out whether Gloria Davy sang the role of Bess or not; on second thought, I don't believe she did, for the woman who sang Bess was a beautiful, light skinned red head who seemed more like a music hall girl than a soprano.

During the intermission, the word *vitalità* uttered by an enthusiastic Italian to a group of friends.

THE MEDIUM (FILM)

I've never seen a single opera by Gian Carlo
Menotti, but have heard fragments on the radio
and saw the film version of *The Medium*.[18]

As far as I can judge, G.C. M[enotti]'s music is
very clever, calculated as it is for dramatic effect,
yet — though it may be very "effective" from this
point of view — is highly mediocre: a sort of sub-
Puccini, youthful thanks to a few injections of
modernism drawn from Stravinsky and others.

When I saw *The Medium,* I found the film capti-
vating for its scenario — which is melodramatic —
and very well done. Also a pleasure to hear people
in modern dress singing. As for the music, due to
our familiarity with the cinema, we listen to it as
if it were a sound track. This is not true when we
hear it on the radio, when it seems totally adequate.
Can we really ask for more, if we already have a
musical *drama*?

THE DEAF MAN'S GLANCE[19]

A strange *tour de force*: a silent opera. That may seem paradoxical, but we are indeed talking about opera here, a pantomimed opera where everything seems to unfold as accompanied by a score – and not even according to a libretto!

You hear this opera with your eyes (to put it that way), and you see it with your ears.

LIANG SHANBO AND ZHU YINGTAI

10/18/55, People's Theater.

The "Shaoxing Opera" *The Loves of Liang Shanbo and Zhu Yingtai,* that I had already seen on film and which today strikes me as an even more wonderful work than I had thought at first, in spite of the strong impression it made on me: a great opera, up there with the best (Verdi, Mussorgsky, etc.). A very measured music, which is unleashed at the end (Zhu Yingtai's dance before the grave of her beloved), just after a few, particularly intense moments corresponding to the main points of the story.

The next to last tableau, a procession — suggested by just a few men carrying lanterns and flags — leading Zhu Yingtai to the wedding ceremony past the tomb with its cupola where Liang Shanbo lies buried; in the orchestra, a noisy march, punctuated by loud blows on the gong. (This is one of the moments where the music and the staging are displayed.)

A final, exquisite tableau (missing in the film, where you see only two butterflies fluttering about): in front of a backdrop of painted flowers, Liang Shanbo and Zhu Yingtai (played by two women, as is the custom with the Shaoxing Opera), wearing costumes that all but hide their sex, dance together like two butterflies, waving long veils. The two unfortunate lovers are united for eternity.

The work ends in a blaze of enthusiasm. Many encores. The performers come back on stage to bow, continuing their dance.

This finale – which is both the conclusion of the drama and a point of contact with the public – recalls certain finales of western operas:

the end of *Don Giovanni,* with the chorus sung facing the public (and before the curtain, with the lights gradually coming on in the hall, in the Aix-en-Provence production), with all the characters announcing what they will do next, now that Don Juan has disappeared into hell;

Falstaff's final fugue, with the moral: "Tutto nel mondo è burla."[20]

It also recalls Guglielmo's direct appeal to the

public in his aria from the second act of *Così fan tutte,* which he sings as if on a stage. And also, the prologue of *I Pagliacci,* sung before the curtain by one of the interpreters (half made-up for the role he will play in the "play within a play").

CHINESE OPERA

According to Messrs Li H'o Tsen and Chang Mo Yuan, assistant director and producer respectively of Troupe #3 of the Peking Classical Theater, met October 24, 1955:

The "Peking Opera," which now represents the essence of Chinese theater, goes back two centuries, and is consequently quite young compared to the traditional theater, which goes back to the age of the Han Dynasty. It utilizes a combination of song, combat, dialogs, and action. If dance was used in the past, as it is today, in conjunction with singing and combat, it was the work of the various protagonists themselves.

The masks – facial paint today – go back more than two thousand years. Under the Han Dynasty, goddess dances were performed by masked dancers, but no scenes were acted or sung.

Dance theater developed under the Tang Dynasty, but separate dancers and singers were employed. During this period, hand gestures such as those used today were added to the singing. While under the Han, the dancers wore long sleeves, under the Tang, the dancers were bare-armed at first, with sleeves beginning at the wrists (and this at court, under Buddhist influence). Masks were worn, especially by warriors, whose combats were inspired by those of the people.

The very long sleeves indicate social status: those who have long sleeves do not work. One proverb says: "Those who have long sleeves dance well." The play of sleeves is strictly determined by the staging. There are two types of sleeves: 1) below the elbow; 2) longer still (used in Shaoxing-style opera, less so in Peking-style since they impede movement).

In general, the historic aspects of the costumes are emphasized, with an accent on traditional details and a tendency to differentiate very clearly between the nobles, rich, and poor, etc.

The make-up is inspired by that of ancient plays that were sung and danced. {Symbolism of colors in the facial paint of certain male characters: white → scheming, sly; red → passionate; black → honest and frank; gold and silver → divine or supernatural nature; other colors (blue, yellow, etc.) → hatred, cruelty. Actors paint their own faces; a beard is added for emphasis.} All of the beauty is expressed in the costumes, the decor serves only to create a successful performance and guarantee the veracity of the play.

Characteristics of the Peking-style opera:

the continuity of the music, even when the curtain is down (loud gong splashes); the great influence of the Mongoloian *Yuen-chi* music on this type of music;

unlike other regional theaters, there is no decor, so that the stage remains a vague, unlimited space; that varies, however, according to the play, and a scene like that of the Mandarin's daughter who feigns madness to escape from the Emperor to whom her father wishes to give her (in the play *Yu Cheou Fong*) can be played in a decor, for it takes place in a bedroom;

theater that basically presents characters from ancient history and draws its inspiration from all regional theaters, of which it is the "fruit"; the conditions of this theater are very favorable for historical plays with combat scenes.

The symbolic gestures (crossing a threshhold, taking up an instrument, etc.) come from the ancient, traditional theater; today the real life of the people of the past is shown, their gestures, their expressions.

Certain plays can be performed in several styles: for example, *The Pavilion of the West* in Shaohing- or Peking-style; *The White Serpent* in Peking or Northern Province-style; *The Oarsman and the Bozine* (Szechwan), *Yu Cheou Fong,* regional plays gathered and perfected by the Peking Classical Opera.

The very important role of Mei Lanfang, for mime, song, and the play of sleeves (which are expressive, not only esthetic), etc. The actor is plunged deeply in the role he is to play.

VOODOO (DANCES AND CHANTS)

"A ballet that, in spite of the disorder that certain possessions can produce and the fever pitch which the dancing – supported by the chorus and drummers – can reach, does *not* have the bacchanalian character that is so frequently attributed to it, but remains thoroughly organized and, in the end, gives the impression of an extraordinarily varied, yet well-balanced show in which the gracious, formal salutations that I have already alluded to (the twirling that evokes images of the European court dances of the 17th and 18th centuries) alternate with typically African choreographic elements, the whole punctuated with violent outbursts and moments of enthusiasm expressed by cries and leaps. A long series of dramatic or comic entrances, whose protagonists are the followers through whom the gods reveal themselves, and in which all genres are mixed: the epic with the Ogoun (warrior spirits), the comic with the Guédé (whose lugubrious character in combination with their obscene jokes recalls the unbridled fantasy of Shakespeare's clowns), the mythic with Damballa Wedo slithering like a serpent, the amorous with the love-smitten Erzulie, the fantastic with certain elements of the ritual called *petro*: blows on the whistle and the whip that I have never heard – during the ceremonies that their sinister inclination differentiates from those of the *rada* ritual – not to mention the famous scene of the hellish hunt in the opera *Der Freischütz* by Carl Maria von Weber, one of the most powerful works of Romantic music, and one of the crowning achievements, certainly, of opera." ([*Les*] *T*[*emps*] *M*[*odernes*], no. 52, February 1950, 1354–1355).[21]

The gesture of exhortation which are often made by the ũgenikõ (both coryphaeus and choirmasters) in voodoo performances: the arms spread and rising, and the body straightening up a bit on spread legs. This gesture, as the expression of all of human desire.

The gracious lady without a nose – due to yaws or syphillis – made this gesture at Lorgina Eloge's place, holding her woven straw hat Jean Bart-style in her right hand: "…One moment, the woman without a nose is visible from behind, singing and urging on her companions, her straw hat in her hand and making the gesture that we (Alfred Métraux and I) have already seen done many times in similar circumstances: arms spread and raised like a conductor who, in a gesture full of breadth and euphoric enthusiasm, has his musicians rise." (10/9/48, evening)[22]

GREEK KARAGHEUZ

During my first trip to Greece – and particularly in Nauplia – I often saw performances of the shadow theater the Greeks call *Karagozios,* which (I believe) derives from the Turkish Karagheuz that Nerval spoke of. It is a very toned-down derivative, from what I've seen, for I have never heard the slightest obscenity in this open air show, compared to what was apparently one of the defining features of their Ottoman homologues.

On a stage a little wider than that of a puppet show you see, in shadow, colorful decors and equally colorful silhouettes that the puppeteer, hidden under the stage, moves with sticks. He speaks for the various characters – as if they were puppets – most of whom are rendered as specific types: the Clown or Punch-like character that is Karagozios himself, the members of his family, the old peasant Barbayorgo, the Athenian, etc. Each one of these characters has its own song that, like a theme in a radio show, heralds his entrance. The music, if I recall, is reduced to a few melodies on the violin or guitar accompanied by sound effects (the clacking of two boards when characters hit or slap each other, etc.). Each character's theme song is supposedly typical of his native region.

In Naupalia, I also saw a play which, as farcical as it was, had moments of grandeur: Karagozios was tormented by a dragon which terrorized him and devoured his children. In the end, Alexander the Great appeared to come to life in a shining suit of armor and challenged the dragon. As the dragon lay dying, defeated by Alexander, he gave Karogozios back the children he had previously devoured.

In Athens in 1939 – while I was there with my friend Claude Laurens – the painter Ghika took us to a working-class neighborhood to see one of the last "Karagozios" which, according to him, was the last one in the capital. It took place in a hall. The puppeteer, whom we met at the end of the performance, was a rather fat man with a big, black mustache. Little boys helped him with the performance, handing him the characters and accessories, and creating the sound effects. At times, he told us, he had to smack his young assistants, since they would get caught up in the action like the spectators, and forget to do their job. The puppeteer seemed quite vigorous and very clever. For me, however, the Athenian performance lacked the charm of the provincial performances which had so captivated me on many an evening in Nauplia.

OPERAS ON FILM

Carmine Gallone is the big specialist.

Regarding a few of these films, nothing to say: the opera is performed before the camera as it would be in reality, the only differences being a close up or two and a few panned shots. That was the case for *Rigoletto,* for example, and for *The Barber of Seville* that I saw a few years ago.

More interesting, *Il Trovatore* (which includes battle scenes and shows the gypsy's story of the child thrown into the fire), *Tosca* (which shows Floria Tosca singing before the queen and, at the beginning of the last act, the shepherd who sings as he leads his sheep along – but perhaps those things shouldn't be shown since the effect of singing from the wings is lost).

Very remarkable, *Madame Butterfly,* seen in Aix-en-Provence in July 1958: the Japanese characters are played by Japanese people (so that the unpleasant masquerade-like quality of the scene is eliminated), the interior scenes (shot with a Japanese technical director) are beautifully done.

One big mistake, *Pagliacci*: the opposition theater/reality collapses entirely, since it is a movie.

After *Madame Butterfly,* I said to Diego Masson that opera on film may well be opera's saving grace, since you can use talented, good-looking actors dubbed by singers (thus resolving certain performance difficulties that have become so great due to our demands as to the physical appearance of the protagonists and decor). He responded that with filmed opera, the notion of the "performance" disappears: the high c or other vocal prowess loses all interest once it becomes possible not to miss it. For the same reason, a sound recording (which, practically speaking, can be perfect since you can always retake a passage until it is right) cannot have the same appeal as a real performance. Diego Masson's reaction is that of a true "opera lover," and clearly shows the difference that exists between an "opera lover" (who goes to the opera a little like the *aficionado* goes to a bullfight) and the music lover.

In a televised *Fidelio* conducted by Karl Böhm but whose producer I've forgotten, these two marvels: the contrasted profiles of [Marcellina] and Jacquino partially overlap when their voices are superimposed; the soldiers' choir shown in profile, such that we see their lips move.

PERIOD PERFORMANCES

We must imagine that Mozart's music, for example, was probably not as well performed in his own time as it is at current festivals, due to the progress made in the area of organology and because good present day performances are in all likelihood more carefully carried out than they were when the composer was less glorious.

We must also consider period styles: we know, for example, that today Wagner's operas are generally performed more slowly than before; those who heard *Pelléas et Mélisande* when it was written say that it is now sung in a more "bel canto" style than before; after one of the extraordinary performances of the *Barber of Seville* at the 1958 Aix festival, Auric accused Giulini of having directed the overture "as if it had been written by Stravinsky." It is certain – and how could it be otherwise – that today old works are more or less performed according to what has been done in music since the period in which the work was written (for example, today's conductors would have a tendancy to emphasize the Wagnerian character of the music at the end of *Norma*, because we know how much *Tristan and Isolde* owes to the work of Bellini).

In 1963, Pierre Boulez directed *Wozzeck* at the Paris Opera, in a vehement, broadly lyric style quite different from the more restrained performances previously heard. Could it be that Alban Berg's music has fallen into the public domain, so we dare to take a more blunt approach when we now perform it?

UNAFFECTED SINGING

Talented sopranos spoiled by affectation: Teresa Stich-Randall (an admirable virtuoso with an unbearable mannerism), Eugenia Zarevska (a beautiful person who makes you wonder – at least when she sings concerts – how she can transform into so hideous a creature, her face marred by contortions).

Conversely, singers exquisite in their simplicity:

Lydia Styx, a soprano I heard a few years ago in Venice in a concert of serial music given at the Vendramin palace. She sang lieder by Anton Webern on poems by Stefan Georg (of which I didn't understand a word) as if they were popular ballads; that's how I came to understand that Webern's music is more than just high mathematics;

Colette Renard, the original *Irma la Douce,* who sang with as little affectation as a woman sitting at home, sewing or ironing*;

* I could add a few more names to these two, and very gladly! Mirella Freni who, for a few years now, has a beautiful so-

A voice simply "emitted" can be so wonderful (cf. the Hungarian tenor Sandor Konnia as I heard him in *Lohengrin*).

---

prano voice and a remarkable technique, but whose singing seems to emanate from her sensibility alone. (9/6/78).

ACTING IN MUSIC

Opera – whether serious or comic – is musical theater, and it is important that it be well performed both theatrically and musically. Satisfactory performances from both a musical and a dramatic point of view are rather rare and deserve the approval of opera lovers. However, the best is only attained when an opera is "acted in the music," if you will, and this can only occur when performers are not content being good actors, but act in complete harmony with the music, as if the acting were rigorously determined by the music.

I recall a few successful examples of this kind: Marisa Morel's *production* of the performances of *Così fan tutte* and *Falstaff* given by her troup at the Gaîté-Lyrique shortly after the Liberation;

La Fanciulla del West as I saw it performed at the San Carlo in Naples (the bass Andrea Monzelli, in the role of the sheriff, loudly shuffling his pack of cards with an occasional flick of the thumb; in the second act, during the big love duet with Maria

Caniglia and Mario del Monaco, the door repeatedly slammed shut and flung open by the swirling snow storm while the orchestra rages);

Carl Ebert's virtually choreographic production of *Falstaff* and *Le Comte Ory,* as given in 1958 at the Théâtre des Nations by the Glyndebourne Festival.

A few male and female singers are naturals in this style, which can be seen as the true style of the opera artist (the style which *justifies* opera by showing that it is more than a mere juxtaposition of musical and dramatic art):

Graziella Sciutti (who is totally unaffected when she sings, and who acts in the *commedia dell'arte* style);

Marcello Cortis (especially when, in the Aix *Don Giovanni,* he paced across the entire stage during the "catalogue aria," and when, also in Aix as Bartolo of the *Barber,* with his right hand he made the gesture of shutting a lock during his first entrance);

Virginia Zeani (who in 1957 at the Théâtre des Nations took the madness scene of *Lucia di Lammermoor* to the level of Chinese theater, moving around on the stage while swirling the two handkerchiefs that she clenched with her finger-tips);

Hans Beirer (in one of *Otello*'s delirium scenes, walking in time in multiple circles and spinning around as if stunned, his hands pressed to his temples);

Kurt Böhme (in the Baron Ochs of the *Rosenkavalier,* stamping his heel on the planks of the stage when the waltz is evoked);

Renato Capecchi (in *Don Giovanni* and in *Così fan tutte*);

Joan Sutherland (*Lucia di Lammermoor* at the Opera, 1960): not one phrase that was not both expressive and musically beautiful, not one attitude that was not both natural and highly stylized, not one movement that was not in rhythm, no grimace even for the most difficult notes.

What *not* to do when staging an opera: illustrate with gestures, acting, or more or less choreographic scenes what the music is more than sufficiently already saying (cf. Barrault's production of *Wozzeck* for the performances at the Paris Opera in November–December 1963).

BETTER THAN GOOD?

In Lucques, in September 1957, an outdoor performance of *Carmen*. Bad singers, except Micaëla (Ofelia di Marco). Orchestra barely audible, limply conducted by Mano Wolff-Ferrari. Ridiculous staging of the procession preceeding the bullfight: an entire *quadrilla* of matadors walking with sorts of flags – their *muletas* – a sword in their right hand, their arm stretched from their side, the tip of the sword pointing at the ground as if for an official salute.

That said, this performance left me with two unforgettable memories:

in the first act, a pretty young girl is selling fruit at the back of the stage. Seen in profile, she does nothing more than be there, for the beauty and poetry of it;

in the last act, when we know that Carmen is about to die, we see her – on the garden side – cross herself, then slowly walk toward Don José, who stands on the courtyard side: Don José disembowels her with his [*navaja*], the blade sweeping from bottom to top, as it is (apparently) done in Spain. All of Mérimée can be found in that single moment…

FORTUNATE COINCIDENCES
AND GAGS

< Hans Beirer, a big, heavy Wagnerian tenor, sings *Othello* at the Paris Opera. In the last act, after Desdemona's murder, he leans with both hands on a high-back chair. The chair gives under his weight and, for a second, it looks like Othello will fall. No calculated stage moves could express in a more striking way the Herculean strength of the Moor and his distracted state.>

In the third act of *La Traviata,* in Genoa, the party at Violetta's friend's place is the occasion for streamers to be thrown and red balloons to be released. During Violetta and Alfredo's stormy argument, one of the balloons, deflating, sinks slowly down and, its string hanging like a plumbline, alights next to Violetta and remains there, like a microphone, and this provokes a few laughs. Seen from a poetic angle, the balloon's silent descent – and its stop at what appears to be the desired height — is an unexpected piece of good luck.

< At the Théâtre des Nations, in Paris in 1959, an excellent performance of the *Marriage of Figaro* in German, by the Frankfurt Opera under the baton of Georg Solti. At the end of the "Military Aria" which concludes the first act, Chérubin, from the back of the stage, tosses his three-cornered hat toward the public. Solti snatches it out of the air with his left hand while still conducting with his right. This (apparently improvised) gag immediately eliminates any distance between the hall and the stage. Crowning a brilliant performance, it is as pleasant as an *adorno* done in good taste by a torero.*>

---

* *Un ballo in maschera,* chorus at the beginning of Scene 3, Act III:

Fervono amori e danze	"The fever of love and dancing
Nelle felici stanze.	Fills these joyous rooms,
Onde la vita è solo	Where life is but
Un sogno lusinghier.	A marvelous dream."

(Antonio Somma, 1859)

Three concerted styles:

> tragic
> lyric
> comic
> + heroic moments.[23]

Wishing – according to Bayreuth custom – to exclude bravos since they are the very opposite of religious contemplation; in fact, wishing to suppress any public intervention and – reducing it to passivity – hinder any real communication between the artists and it (communication, by definition, cannot be unilateral), does this not come down to stripping the theatrical event of its "ritual party" aspect: this noisily demonstrated communion.[23]

184

OPERA AND CELEBRATION

From a technical view point alone, the relationship between opera (which is drama, music and dance) and the "primitive" spectacle incorporated into a ceremonial.

From a sociological point of view, opera is the spectacle for which the public is still most likely to get dressed up. This undoubtedly because a theatrical performance without music would simply not seem like a celebration.

Mallarmé and the importance of lustre in the theater (cf. *Le Livre* edited by [Jacques] Scherer[24]). Nerval and the "suitor's fine clothes" (cf. *Sylvie*).

Appropriateness of French opera at a time when ballet was one of its indispensable ingredients: if there is no celebration without music, there is not one without dance, either.

The additional necessity of an erotic element, whether explicit (as in Strauss' *Salome*) or implicit (as in traditional operas with romantic plots). The ballet, as a presentation of dancing women, is a direct intervention of eroticism in opera. (A childhood memory: before the First World War, the orchestra section of the Paris Opera packed with gentlemen in black suits who could be seen taking out their lorgnettes when the ballet began; — besides, we know that subscribers had the privilege of access to the dancers' foyer.)

Objection to the French conception of opera as a lyric drama including a ballet: the ballet is but an intermediary added after the fact and dance is not truly integrated in the spectacle.

On the one hand, those who have made a celebration of the opera (Mozart, Verdi, etc.); on the other, those who have made it a mass (Wagner, — indeed, Debussy, in that *Pelléas* is ever so slightly what Cocteau called music "to be listened to with one's head in one's hands").

The superiority of older concert halls over newer ones: overly functional, the latter are no longer fit for a celebration.

The "celebration" in the opera itself: the ball (end of Act 1) and the dinner in *Don Giovanni,* the masquerade ball with which *Un ballo in maschera* ends, the rite of the *Prophet* and the crowning of

Boris Godounov, the "dance of the Hours" in *La Gioconda,* the singing contest in the *Meistersinger,* the peasant ball in *Wozzeck,* the marriage in *Lucia di Lammermoor,* the dinner at the home of Violetta and the last sounds of carnival in *La Traviata,* whose very theme is the "celebration," the Christmas Eve in the Quartier Latin in *La Bohème,* the shepherds' celebration in *Orfeo,* the shooting contest in *Der Freischütz,* the celebration at the inn in *Peter Grimes,* the student wildlife and party at which Olympia performs in *Les Contes d'Hoffmann,* the celebration at the home of the Capulets in *Romeo et Juliette,* and the kermess in *Faust,* the cabaret and corrida scenes in *Carmen,* two balls (Act ii, tableau 1 and Act iii, tableau 1) in *Eugene Onegin.*

OPERA AND BULLFIGHTING

Seeing the torero Victoriano de la Serna in Marseille in one of his better moments, I mentally hummed the waltz of the *Rosenkavalier* as I watched him work the bull with a slightly deliquescent grace.

When he appeared for the first time in Nîmes, the young Mexican torero Fermin Rivera made me think of Rossini, with his vigorous, alert style.

André Castel once introduced me to an old *aficionada* from Nîmes: Mme Cantier. I was amused by the Beethovian tone with which she recalled a "great *faena*" by Juan Belmonte during I don't remember which Spanish *feria* she attended in the company of our common friend. "It made us sick…" she said, like a Mme Verdurin rudely shaken by Vinteuil's Sonata.

Musical intervention — as a homage or encouragement to the torero — right in the middle of the corrida. How astounding these *paso doble* are, danced arias punctuating a tragedy.

OPERA AND GASTRONOMY

In Aix-en-Provence at one of the festivals, André Masson and I amused ourselves an entire evening by imagining the food or drink – and, if possible, both – most appropriate for the dinner before and the light meal after the performance of every famous opera we knew.

Of course, such simple associations as beer and sauerkraut for Wagner's operas, chianti and pasta for Verdi's, manzarella et paella for *Carmen,* etc., are to be avoided. Rather, I'd like to determine the beverage or dish that actually responds to the character of the work, and that's much more difficult!

Could you say that, generally speaking, champagne and nutritious but light dishes (grilled meat or fish) would be most appropriate for Mozart's operas? That *Pelléas et Mélisande* would call for a vegetarian menu accompanied by cool water? As for the great historic operas, they would be adapted to rich, complex menus with several wines. And *Carmen* would require a wine, generous of course, but less vigorous than a manzarella (a lambrusco, for example, or a fendant) and, for solid food, one of these dark, raw hams appealing for their extreme density.

I understood "tournedos Rossini" when I ate some in Mantua, at the restaurant Les Garibaldini: there, they prepare them with white truffle (which gives them more aroma) and, rather than present them as a luxury dish, they give the impression of more of an honest, peasant dish. Figaro, a man of the people, could well eat *those* tournedos!

Saturday, June 2, 1962, the last performance of *Don Pasquale* by the Teatro Massimo de Palerme at the Théâtre des Champs-Elysées. In the front row, seated between a rather old and rather young, pretty woman (probably his wife and daughter), Roger Topolinsky, owner of the restaurant La Pérouse, with the face of a bearded *gourmand,* the tall stature and corpulence of a *bon vivant.* All three very enthusiastic, which makes me think of Stendhal, of Rossini's legendary gourmandise, etc.

SUPERSTARS

There aren't any more (or so it seems) except among movie stars and opera singers: James Dean and his fate, Callas and her escapades.

In France, with its system of repertory opera companies, singers are more or less state employees (without being "national artists" as in Eastern European countries). Italian singers, on the other hand, lead a life closer to that of touring artists. Artist restaurants like the Café de la Scala in Milan or the Pizzaria da Ciro, Via Santa Brigida (near the Galleria) in Naples. At the Pizzaria da Ciro I saw Rigoletto (Carlo Tagliabue) eating with his daughter (the young Antonietta Pastori) after the performance, then Tagliabue greeted by the kitchen staff with their big hats, all dressed in white. At the same place, when we were there together, the coat lady always called René Leibowitz "maestro" (since he had given her his score and baton after a rehearsal). Also saw Vittorio Guy the conductor presiding over a lunch that nearly included the whole troupe that was to give *The Magic Flute* just a few days later (when the maestro left, the singers began acting like school children, flinging little bread balls across the table at each other). A few years before, I had seen the conductor Gabriele Santini, after another performance of *La Fanciulla del West,* remind the bass Andrea Monzelli, who was eating an enormous portion of spaghetti, that there would be a performance the following day, and that he should show a little restraint.

The Italian public's taste for opera and the less than homebody life lead by performers certainly tend to make the latter as susceptible as any stage actor to become "superstars."

Note also the following habit of the working class public of Italian opera: as soon as the intermission has begun, they rush down to the orchestra pit to look at the musicians and maybe even speak with them.

MAURICE RENAUD (at the Opéra-Comique)
As a child, I was taken to see *The Flying Dutchman* at the Opéra Comique, with Maurice Renaud

whom my mother ardently admired. Marthe Chenal was his partner. I knew I was going there to hear a "great artist," and a complete artist who acted as well as he sang.

I remember his emaciated face, his absent gaze and the seemingly petrified stillness that he gave to the character of the Dutchman. Chenal seemed pretty coarse next to him (but this judgement may be rooted in a certain prejudice of my parents, having previously heard our cousin by marriage Claire Friché sing the role, with the same Maurice Renaud).

Having heard a few phonograph recordings of Maurice Renaud (in particular, an aria from [*Sigurd*]), I rather clearly recall his voice and the way he sang. A very smooth baritone, with a very flowing style, very even and always perfectly musical. Tito Gobbi, when he simply sang "bel canto," without dramatic effects, reminded me of this style.

Another time, I was taken to the Opera to hear him sing *Hamlet*. But he was replaced by a one Henri Dangès who (if I recall) had a certain talent but was nevertheless a second-rate singer. Not ready to admit that we had lost out in the exchange, I found Henri Dangès magnificient. Having heard him in other roles (like Valentin in *Faust*), I wrote a little poem about him — "You whose charming voice…" (the only fragment I still remember from this eulogy) — and sent it to him. Kindly, he responded by sending two autographed photos, in postcard format, showing him in the role of Hamlet.

In an old issue of *Musica* I read that Maurice Renaud, when he played the role of Herod in Massenet's *Hérodiade,* insisted on making his own costume and that, to do so, he documented it thoroughly for maximum archeological accuracy.

VANNI MARCOUX (Paris Opera)
The last example of the French/Italian singer, as were the baritone Victor Maurel and, I believe, a few others.

< As a child, I heard him in a Verist opera by [Ermanno] Wolf-Ferrari, *Les Joyaux de la Madone.* He played the role of a pimp or Neopolitan bad boy. In the first act you could see him in a trattoria, very realistically eating a plate of spaghetti and singing with perfect ease. >

Later, I heard him in *Boris Godounov* in which, though he didn't have a huge voice, he cut an impressive figure. I must have heard him as Mephisto in *Faust,* as well, and (perhaps) as Iago in *Othello.*

A few years ago, while he was director of the Bordeaux Opera, I heard a radio interview with him on the occasion of I don't remember which gala. Nearly voiceless, but with great style, he sang a few measures of the pretty aria from *Falstaff* in Italian: "When I was the the Lord of Norfolk's page...." I believe that *Falstaff* was one of his great successes.

MAX LORENTZ (at the Paris Opera)

It was in *Tristan* that I heard him for the first time.

His worn, veiled voice that seems to tear at his throat as it comes out but – as he uses it with great style – moves you such that you'd think it issued from deep within him and only painfully came to the surface.

His stature as a tragedian and his way of walking – with big, slow, heavy steps that nevertheless have a certain springiness – a size and gait on par with the enormous stage.

The same, as Aegistheus in *Elektra* at the Vienna Opera (September 1960). Now nearly voiceless, it is only with great effort that he occasionally emits a goat-like bleating, as if to remind the spectator who might otherwise forget, that singing, not declamation, is what opera is all about. His physical presence and acting are still so impressive, his articulation and rhythm so perfect, that the word "decline" doesn't even come to mind.

TITO GOBBI (at the Thermes de Caracalla)

His incredible physical and vocal authority were obvious as soon as – singing Tonio in *I Pagliacci* – he spread the curtain and, standing on the proscenium, wrapped in a great black cloak, began the famous prologue.

Then his entrance, with the mule-drawn cart of itinerant actors. Hobbling along, he crosses the entire breadth of the stage. At that very moment (I believe), I was sure I was feeling the same thing as those people who saw Frédérick Lemaître in a highly colorful role, like *Robert Macaire*.

RENATA TEBALDI (at the San Carlo of Naples)
Joan of Arc [in Verdi's *Giovanna d'Arco*] listened
to celestial and infernal voices, and heard herself
damned by her father. We saw her with the King
before the Reims cathedral (with an apparently
life-size reproduction of the entire façade) and,
her dagger at her side against her long medieval
robe, she kissed Charles VII on the lips in a supposedly French garden. We saw her in prison, then
dead on a cot between her father and the king who
stood lamenting, mid-stage, surrounded by an
army of choral singers or walk-ons dressed in
white. Now, with a flashing smile, she bows under
the applause like a good girl proud of her success,
robust and fresh as a canteen woman.

The same, in *Aïda,* at the Paris Opera.
Something like Fausto Coppi, as I saw him in
Cannes, just before the arrival of one stage of the
Tour de France: face dry and relaxed, hair well
combed and slicked down, well ahead of the bulk
of his competitors, all of them perspiring, hag-
gard and dusty. Her voice easily dominates an even
tumultuous orchestra, and occasionally diminishes,

with no solution of continuity, in perfectly distinct yet never timbreless *pianissimi*. A single resonant legato, which is constantly musical and passes in tone from grave to shrill, from veiled to brilliant without stumbling. At emotional moments, you can hear her breathe. Responding to ovations, she bows, a good girl, her hand addressing the public with little, impish gestures.

BORIS CHRISTOFF (at the Paris Opera)
The curtain rises, having closed on the madness of Boris Godounov. The other Boris – Christoff, the bass – apparently can't manage not being Godounov any longer. The ovations leave him bent over, his gaze lost somewhere. Little by little, he seems to recover. We see him slowly straighten up, then respond to the ovation by throwing kisses to the public with both hands, one of which is covered with rings.

MARIA MENEGHINI CALLAS
La Traviata was being given in a matinee performance that Sunday at La Scala in Milan, and, right before the performance, we were having lunch at

the Café de la Scala. From morning, the city around the theater seemed to be bubbling over, just like the arena neighborhood of a Spanish city right before a corrida. A lot of people had come by bus and a crowd swarmed around the ticket windows. Occasionally, a uproar was heard, though we could never understand why. Toward the end of our meal, the waiters of the café lowered the metal curtain as if they feared a riot.

She's the one who keeps the others from sleeping: according to *her,* Schwarzkopf has also been losing weight; Tebaldi (as she appeared in Paris in *Aïda*) was obviously more self-conscious than she had been previously. She seems to have ushered in a new type of soprano and her colleagues have to take that into account, like Joselito and the old-fashioned toros had to modify their style when Belmonte appeared.

Her unpopularity among many Italians. In Venice in 1959, I heard a lady call her "bruta." At the time of the Onassis scandal, a young porter at the Grand Hotel told us she was haughty ("she won't even look at us"), and on the contrary, praises Mme Onassis who is at least nice and pretty. The young porter makes us a drawing to show us just how ugly Callas' legs are. According to him, she never would have made it without her husband.

The recording she made of *Madame Butterfly* under the baton of Herbert von Karajan. Her voice, less padded than Tibaldi's, is more appropriate for the role, which is not that of a woman, but of an adolescent. Moreover – a personal interpretation or an indication from Karajan ? – she sings a bit in the Mélisande style: little lyric turgidity but rather, a "flat" melody. With this treatment, Butterfly's Japanism resembles the Pre-Raphaelism that marks *Pelléas* and other works by Debussy.

Superiority (the only one, but how important) of Callas over Tebaldi: whereas the latter is always Tebaldi marvelously [using] her marvelous voice, the former is capable of being different from herself in each role she sings. A bit like the great toreros of the past, able to do non-standard *faenas* tailored to each of the bulls they had to fight.

In June 1964, Maria Callas came to sing *Norma* at the Paris Opera, an attempt, perhaps, to prove that she is indeed able to sing this role. She pulls it off – but just barely so – thanks to her extraordinary presence, her intelligent, impulsive acting, and her gaze which (Monique Lévi-Strauss points out to me) so sets her apart from other sopranos, who almost always have "eyes like a dead fish." But what holes in her voice, and notes that are screamed and at best approximate! The aria "Casta diva," sung almost entirely in veiled tones, is literally sidestepped; you can see that she really has to control herself to end brilliantly. Triumphant success, undoubtedly orchestrated, with an insistant claque, numerous bouquets thrown onto the stage, etc. A viperine allure which, for all that, is fitting for the role; often, an ironic smile; noble posturing, cut with impetuous movements. You'd think she was fighting with the other characters as well as with the public. The fact is that in spite of her shortcomings, she is "unique" in the strict meaning of that term.

NEW GENRE

An endless stream of recordings and festivals tends to make boring stars of the most talented singers. Even in the world of "classical" music, there are now recorded *best sellers*: Callas, Tebaldi, Mario del Monaco, etc. Singers with less commercial potential seem literally like poor relations next to these lions and lionesses; they are hardly exported, and rarely appear in collections of "great recordings," so that you have to go out of your way to hear them.

The terrible thing about these festivals at which, for financial reasons, few new works are ever performed, and which impel everyone to give the best performance – guarenteed in writing – of a few famous operas.

Everything is tied to the development of tourism, and of the recording and radio industry.

The ridiculous policy of the Paris Opera which is all too often satisfied to hire a huge international star for a few performances (which is insufficient all the same) of this or that work chosen from among the most hackneyed.

MONSIEUR GASTON

Visiting the La Scala Museum in Milan with René and Mary-Jo L[eibowitz], we had a French-speaking guide. In one of the rooms of the museum, he showed us the passageway leading to La Scala. When L[eibowitz] asked him if we could visit the concert hall, he replied it was impossible, since there was a rehearsal going on at the time. As we were leaving, he changed his mind and told us to come back to see him and ask for "Monsieur Gaston." Two or three mornings in a row, he surreptitiously ushered us into a box. Hiding in the back of the box (for he didn't want us to be seen), we attended some of the rehearsals of *Boris Godounov*. In particular, we would see Gino Penno, in the role of Dmitri, sing his aria from the act of the revolt: on horseback, wearing a gray suit and glasses.

The wonderful character of these hidden passageways leading to concert halls or theaters: Hoffmann's tale about *Don Juan* (the inn in which the bedroom reserved for distinguished guests leads to one of the boxes in the theater); in the old Palais du Trocadéro, there was such a passageway leading from the Ethnographic Museum to one of the boxes in the theater.

It also reminds me of the rabbit leading Alice through the rabbit hole/tunnel that takes her to Wonderland. A story I read as a child — it was in the *Livres roses pour la jeunesse,* a collection published by Larousse — also tells of a modern girl in a house with a sort of gallery (as if hung with paintings, mirrors, or displays), a gallery of tableaux or scenes each of which makes up one episode and corresponds perhaps to one of the days of the week. Could it be a gallery opening on a series of bedrooms? or wonderful transformations sparked by real elements of the decor: a mirror, flames from the hearth, flowers or foliage that adorns the walls? This is one of those tales that had a profound effect on me when I read them as a child, but the fact is I have nearly forgotten it.

In September 1959, I was in Venice with Z[ette] and the Leibowitz' and, taking the *vaporetto* to go from Santa Maria del Giglio to the Rialto, I found myself sitting to the right of a tall, heavy-set man who was dressed like an average tourist (gray, flannel-like pants, tweed-like jacket of indistinct color). He had a small radio on his lap – it was playing the Italian news. In his bovine repose, he didn't seem to be listening to it. He had a little mustache and I saw, in profile, his red face and his remarkably flat nose. I recognized "Monsieur Gaston," all alone, and most likely there on vacation.

In March 1960, visiting the "Museum of the Theater" once again, I caught a glimpse of Monsieur Gaston, his face flush and moronic.

HOFFMANNIAN EVENINGS

On September 13, 1958, for the centenary of Puccini's birth, a performance of *Turandot* at Pistoia's Teatro Manzoni. The Massons, Z[ette] and I traveled there by car, from Montecatini Terme where I was taking the waters.

A pleasant dinner at the *ristorante* Nando, which is on the ground floor of an 18th century palace. Then we walked to the Teatro Manzoni.

The building, which currently serves as both a theater and movie house, dates from approximately 1800. Its facade has been modified, but it is nearly intact on the inside. Below, 24 boxes numbered 1–25 in great, gilded numbers are visible from the hall; in place of the non-existant box number 13, you have access to the central aisle of the orchestra section. Above the stage, hanging over the center, a clock with a moving face sports two cupids, one of whom points to the time with his index finger. The foyer of the theater – a huge hall on the ground floor – communicates with the little, (very modern) neighboring bar, which serves as a buffet and opens on the street.

A weak performance for more than one reason, but organized in an excellent movement and cleverly staged, with limited means. The role of the slave Liù was sung, quite well, by a rather young (or so it seemed) soprano: Elena Todeschi.

After Liù's death, a "minute of silence" and the orchestra stands, to mark the moment where Puccini's score — later finished by his disciple Alfano — comes to an end. The two performers then on stage — Prince Calaf at the rear, back to the public, and Turandot, front right, facing the public — stand absolutely still.

Two or three days before, in the main café of the city, we had asked the waiter if the sort of *palio* called "Celebration of the Bear" (which we had attended the preceeding year) had taken place. The waiter's reply: "Last year it was the Celebration of the Bear, this year the opera…"

Puccinian performances in Lucca, at the Teatro del Giglio: *Manon Lescaut* (September 14), *Madame Butterfly* (September 17).

In Lucca, Puccini's home town, the theater, the Universo Hotel with its restaurant, and the *ristorante* Giglio (whose decor, both very simple and very "Italian palace," is as wonderful as the food) can be found on the same square, la Piazza del Giglio, in a part of which the lotto game is held at nightfall.

Very good performance of *Manon Lescaut,* with an admirable staging and one of the best tenors we had ever heard, Carlo Bergonzi, who is always musical even at climactic moments. The act at the inn, with students and bourgeois in their three-cornered hats, and couples strolling by in the background, reminds one of the frescos of Tiepolo the son (*La Vie en rose, Le Nouveau Monde*) that can be seen in the Cà Rezzonico in Venice. The second act evokes a libertine 18th century, without sentimental mush (a series of romantic scenes, concluded by the villainous pillage of the jewels). The call and boarding of the girls at the port in Le Havre onto the great sailing ship evoke l'abbé Prévost as much as the Defoe of *Moll Flanders.* The end in Louisana, with the two protagonists wandering in a desert landscape, was realized with great emotion.

At the beginning of the afternoon of September 17, we settled into the Hotel Universo, which we were to leave the following day for Orvieto. By the end of the afternoon, the posters for the theater sported a green band covering the white band announcing that *Madame Butterfly* — tentatively scheduled for the 16 — was put off to the 17 due to the slight indisposition of the *prima donna* Antonietta Stella, now announced that Stella would be replaced by one Orietta Moscucci. The Hotel Universo turned out to be an "opera hotel" as there are "bullfighting hotels": conductors, singers (one of whom, the mezzo, sucked on little candies to clear her throat), other employees of the theater and simple opera lovers sit next to one another at dinner time. Dinner at the restaurant Giglio, much better and much prettier than the hotel's. We were refused, with excuses, a table by the window; it was to be given to four people, one of whom is a very pretty, very dark-haired woman and (we were told) the two main performers of *Manon Lescaut,* whom we recognized to be Clara Patrella and Carlo Bergonzi. During the performance, Orietta Moscucci proved to be a good singer and a great actress. She and the mezzo singing Suzuki had perfectly assimilated the gestures and attitudes — indeed even in the way they moved — of actresses from the Far East. The beauty, for example, of Butterfly's slender hands applied to the paper screen as she waits.

The Hotel Marino e della Scala, in Milan: all you have to do it cross the street to go to the "Café del Teatro," a few meters more and you're at the "Teatro della Scala." The bar of the Marino, frequented in the evening by what must be prostitutes.

AN OPERA EVENING
IN SAN GIMIGNANO

In August 1947, I was spending the summer in Si-
enna with Z[ette], living at the Palazzo Ravizza,
Piano degli Mantellini, a small, old palace whose
owners – the Grottanelli's – had transformed it
into a *pensione*. That summer, which was not the
first one I had spent in Italy (since I had already
summered in Pallanza on Lake Maggiore in 1929, I
believe), but which nevertheless inaugurated a series of such Italian summers, I was fortunate enough
to attend a performance of *La Traviata* given on the
Piazza del Duomo in San Gimignano.

The stage was set up in the very tight space of the
arched doorway to the ancient palace of the Podestat,
a building dating from the 13th–14th centuries (according to the guide), flanked by a tower and pierced
on the second floor by three Romanesque windows.
The orchestra (without a pit, obviously) and ground
seats filled the square, and the front steps of the
cathedral facing the palace served as the balcony.

Good singers: Onelia Fineschi, Nicola [Filacuridi], Piero Guelfi. An obviously local orchestra, conducted by one *maestro* Strano who wore a white jacket and conducted in the café-music style (which, without really being good, was nevertheless much better than the heavy conducting style of our Parisian *maestros*).

In the course of the performance, a dog happened to cross the square, between the orchestra and the ground seats.

During the interminable intermissions, the supporting male actors and chorus members cooled off at the Romanesque windows, or smoked cigars.

The performance ended about 2 AM and we returned by car to the Palazzo Ravizza with the few of the *pensione*'s other clients who had come with us: a young Italian girl, little more than an adolescent really, who was studying the piano with the hope of becoming a concert pianist; a young English student, likable yet impertinent, like so many of his compatriots; and others that I have forgotten.

In our room, a meal was waiting for us. We did it great honor.

AT THE CASINO D'ENGHIEN

For the past few years, the Casino d'Enghien has been giving a sort of small summer festival which includes a few performances of Italian and – sometimes – German or Viennese opera.

It was there that I saw *La Forza del destino, Norma,* and the *Zauberflöte,* then, in 1959 and in 1960, a performance by the charming opera company from Como (which doesn't include a single "star," but people who do their best under generally intelligent musical direction and production) of *Lo Fratre 'nnamorato,* a comic opera by Pergolesi, then Puccini's *Le Triptyque* (a veritable anthology of the various Puccinian styles: Verist, lyrical, comical).

The proximity of Enghien Lake, surprising for its Helvetic aspect after the suburban trek. A public who for the most part – dressed up a bit more than usual for the opera – played the "water city" or "festival" game.

The last season – summer 1960 – attending the *Triptyque* with a few friends, we discovered a little restaurant/bar just a few steps from the theater (on the sidewalk opposite the Casino, and a little to the left). It is to the Casino d'Enghien what the Biffi-Scala and the Pizzeria da Ciro are to La Scala and to the San Carlo, respectively. We ate there after the show, while nearly the entire company had dinner in the next room. More than a pompous performance with a brilliant cast, an evening like that one is the "piece of luck" which true "opera lovers" always hope for…

[Compare] the performances given in 1946, at the Gaîté-Lyrique by Marisa Morel and a few of her colleagues from La Scala who were not yet rehabilitated: *Così fan tutte, Falstaff.* Excellent conductor (Otto Ackermann) and a few excellent singers (Giulietta Simionato, Suzanne Danco, Marcelle [Cortis]…) The nice "whatever means we have" nature of these performances.

THE OPERA OF ROME
AT THE CARACALLA THERMAL BATHS

The monument (made of brick, with two huge, standing walls that frame the stage). The crowd that stretches as far as the eye can see (and straight outside the enclosure). The stage preparations in the darkness behind the ramp of huge spotlights aimed at the audience to blind them (a lot of people on the plateau, men and women performers, stagehands and electricians, people in work clothes and singers in costumes, occasionally a male or female dancer trying out a move, all of them barely visible and nearly imagined). The strange cell of light in which the stage is inscribed during the performance. The dark, starry night, with an occasional passing plane with an annoying drone. The contingent of guards on horseback that you see — and hear — trot off at the end of the show.

A PILGRIMAGE TO MECCA

When I stayed there for nearly two weeks in 1960, I was convinced: the true capital of Opera is Vienna, not Milan, as I had previously believed.

In Vienna, the opera lover's only problem is that the choice is too great. There are two Opera houses open each evening, not to mention the Sunday matinées: Stadtsoper (with *opera seria* performances that rival those of La Scala); Volksoper (specializing in Viennese opera); in addition, two or three times a week there are performances (also of exceptional quality) of Mozartian or other operas at the Redoutensaal, a little 18th century (?) hall which is part of the Residence complex, right next to the Spanish Merry-Go-Round.

At the Sacher Hotel (whose namesake – and, I believe, founder – was Metternich's cook, who, at the famous congress during which the Holy Alliance was created, invented the chocolate cake that can still be found in all Viennese pastry shops under the name "Sacher torte"), the room we had, on the 4th or 5th floor, opened on the studios of the Stadtsoper where, each evening, we saw young male or female ballerinas in their work tights (in the studio to the right of us) or else a few singers rehearsing some scene whose movements seemed choreographically determined.

In Vienna, opera lovers are so numerous that it is impossible for tourists to get tickets, except on the black market. It is easiest to place an order through the hotel porter.

At the Stadtsoper, behind the rows of ground-floor seats, there is a promenade gallery thronged with crowds of mostly young people, many of whom carry field binoculars. Here opera is apparently one of the *necessities of life*. That doesn't mean that people are true dilettantes. Gluttons rather than gourmets, they fill the concert halls no matter what opera is given, abandoning themselves in the most impetuous ovations and – if necessary – hailing a performer who sang badly with bravos.

Each evening before we went to bed and, most often, on leaving the Stadtsoper, we stopped by the Sacher café where a number of people,

Viennese or others, were doing like us; just like the Parisians of the past would go drink hot chocolate at the Café Prévost when they left the Opéra or the Opéra-Comique.

OPERA AND FOLKLORE

Everyone knows that opera makes use of folklore. The Russians didn't wait for Zhdanov to implement pro-folklore arguments and, for their part, the Italian Verists were also inspired by folklore.

Rarer is the contrary which, rather than going from folklore to opera, goes from opera to folklore. By that I mean those things which make opera a creator of folklore, and not simply a purveyor of popular music, through the classic process of the popularization of sophisticated music. I can give two precise examples of this: the fact that now, in Mantua, one can visit not only the house of Rigoletto and the inn of Sparafucile but, at the Ducal Palace, among the portraits of the Gonzagas hangs that of the Duke of Mantua of *Rigoletto*; that fact that the overture of *Carmen* has become (practically without modification) a *de rigueur* performance piece in many of the plazas throughout southern France.

< In Vizzini (Sicily), the square of the *Cavalleria rusticana* is reproduced on post cards. But I don't know whether that goes back to the work of Verga or to that of Mascagni.

In the gorges of Frauchard (in the Fontainebleau forest) a passage through the rocks is called the "Norma passage."

In Nagasaki, Japan, one can visit a "house of Butterfly.">

ART AND LIFE

"{July 8, 1957.} What, in short, I have been wanting to do for a while: put a little Italian opera in
my life. It began about the time I spoke of the "liq-
uidation of love in Verdi's operas," or the liquida-
tion of the esthete mind that allowed me to be
satisfied with love experienced through opera. I
could never have one program for art and another
for life. Art is not a *distraction* but a *transfiguration*
of life; it must be integrated into life and not
merely embellish it, like a superfluous ornament.
I once jokingly said to C... that, with all it takes
to live Italian opera; why would anyone want to
listen to it?"[25]

How the Marcellus Theater in Rome illustrates
a desirable fusion of theater and life! Houses stand
on what was once a place for spectacles. Compare, in Lucques, the Market Square established
on the site of an amphitheater which has entirely

disappeared, except for the ellipsis formed by the houses. Toward the beginning of the last century, within the arenas of Nîmes there were (apparently) houses.

WHAT WE WERE LOOKING FOR
SO FAR AWAY

Antonin Artaud and others after him have praised Balinese theater, Japanese theater, Chinese theater, and God knows what else! In a word, these exotic theaters which – compared to the poverty of our Western theater – appear to be examples of *total* theater. In these Eastern theaters, performers have style and rhythm; they are both actors and dancers, and sound plays an actual role in the drama, rather than being merely "sound effects."

Now, we just so happen to have at hand – in Europe, even – a typical example of this total theater. I'm thinking of *opera,* which has been so terribly discredited, precisely by those very same "avant-garde" figures who turned to the East for their teachings. Isn't opera an entirely rhythmic, stylized form of theater? A form of theater in which spectacle, music and pure drama work on the emotions of a spectator invested with what is offered him as exactly as he would be in a "theater of cruelty"?

That so few are aware of this is explained by the fact that, practically speaking, opera is almost never performed as it should be. Too often, if not poorly sung, at the very least poorly acted or performed in a style which is not that of the opera, such a purely dramatic style that the demands of rhythm seem to be forgotten.

A revolution necessarily inscribed within the context of a specific civilization being nothing less than a transformation of something that already exists, shouldn't those Western men of the theater, who dream of a revolution that would restore dignity to our theater, take into consideration the possible point of departure opera offers us – to renovate, of course! but by attempting to retain the essence of what it proposes?

To the degree that it *can* be this total theater, is opera not, of all theatrical forms, the most worthy of being served?

WHAT I FIND IN OPERA

Esthetic pleasure in its pure state, in an ambiance of celebration — a real *dilettante's* pleasure.

That I expect this unadulterated pleasure from opera (an appreciation of *beauty* alone, outside of any philosophical or moral considerations) may explain why a light work — a comic opera, for example — can move me more than a tragic work: I know that this light work offers me opera in all its purity, hence an emotional quality much finer than when sentimental or intellectual elements are mixed with it. It is, in sum, as if I needed a *frivolous* opera (a work of celebration and pleasure) to unveil for me the exact nature of opera, and as if this unveiling (and not the content of the work) were the motive for the emotion.

NOTES

1 [*Musique d'ameublement* or "furniture music" was intended by Satie to be the quintessential background music, so discreet as to be inaudible. More ambient than musical, it was to serve the same purpose "as lighting, heating and *comfort* in all its forms." The first performance of "furniture music," composed by Satie and Darius Milhaud, took place at the Galerie Barbazanges on the Faubourg Saint-Honoré on March 8, 1920, during the intermission of *Ruffian, toujours; truand, jamais,* a play by Max Jacob; the public was instructed not to listen.]

2 This cantata, commissioned by Paul Rivet and Georges Henri Rivière – respectively director and assistant director of the Musée d'ethnographie du Trocadéro which, in 1937, would become the Musée de l'homme – was premiered on January 17, 1938 at the Ecole normale de musique de Paris.

3 Cf. Guillaume Apollinaire, "Souvenirs" in *Calligrammes* (Paris: Gallimard [Pléiade], 1965, p 299).

4 Written on a seperate sheet of paper inserted after "The Lively Hell."

5 Zette was the diminutive of Louise (*née* Godon), Michel Leiris' wife.

6 Also known as *La Fida Ninfa,* composed in 1732.

7 Cf. Charles Baudelaire, from "Phares," in *Les Fleurs du Mal:* "Delacroix, lac de sang hanté par des mauvais anges, / Ombragé par un bois de sapins toujours verts, / Où sous un ciel chagrin, des fanfares étranges / Passent, comme un

soupir étouffé de Weber." [from "Beacons" in *Les Fleurs du Mal*: "Delacroix, bloody lake haunted by evil angels, / In the shade of a pine wood ever-green, / Where, beneath a sorrow sky, strange fanfares / Pass, like Weber's stifled sigh."]

8   Allusion to Plautus' comedy, *The Menaechmus Twins,* which tells the adventures of twin brothers, a subject notably used by Shakespeare (*Comedy of Errors*) and by Tristan Bernard (*The Brighton Twins*).

9   Cf. Alan Lomax, *Mister Jelly Roll* (New York: Duell, Sloan and Pearce, 1950).

10 Written on a separate sheet of paper.

11 This is Daisy S..., the "Kay" evoked at length in *L'Age d'homme* (Paris: Gallimard, [1939], 1973, [collection "Folio"]), 159–182.

12 Cf. Jean Racine, *Phèdre*, I.3.

13 This is a typed draft of the long note written for a new edition of *L'Age d'homme* in 1964 (cf. *L'Age d'homme, op. cit.,* 1973, 212–214).

14 *Die Dreigroschenoper,* German film made in 1930 by Georg Wilhelm Pabst with Rudolf Forster, Carola Neher and Lotte Lenya.

15 [In *Alcools* (Paris: Gallimard [Pléiade], 1965), p 105]

16 The former assistant director of the Musée d'ethnographie du Trocadéro, founder in 1937, and first conservator of the Musée des Arts et Traditions populaires, Georges Henri Rivière (1897–1985) was the directly responsible for Michel Leiris' career as an ethnographer. It was thanks to him that Leiris participated in the famous Dakar–Djibouti mission

directed by Marcel Griaule from 1931 to 1933, and during which he kept a diary which, published in 1934, became *L'Afrique fantôme.*

17 *The Gay Divorcee,* an American film made in 1934 by Mark Sandrich, with Fred Astaire and Ginger Rogers.

18 *The Medium,* Anglo-Italian film made in 1951 by Gian Carlo Menotti, with Marie Powers, Anna Maria Alberghetti and Leo Coleman.

19 Play by Bob Wilson, first performed in France at the Nancy Festival in 1971.

20 "All is but a farce."

21 Self-quotation of a passage from the article "Martinique, Guadeloupe, Haiti," published in *Les Temps modernes,* 1950, no. 52, 1345–1368.

22 Extract from Michel Leiris' travel diaries, *Martinique/ Guadeloupe (1948),* manuscripts no. 44 and no. 47.

23 Loose page and card inserted after this section by Michel Leiris.

24 *Le « Livre » de Mallarmé* (Paris: Gallimard, 1957).

25 From Leiris' *Journal 1922–1989,* which he quotes here.

Index

Abravanel, Maurice de, 151
Ackermann, Otto, 215
Africaine, (L'), 57
Age d'homme, (L'), 134, 136
Aïda, 27, 50, 54, 57, 124, 142, 197
Alfano, Franco, 57, 137, 139, 208
Andrea Chénier, **143–144**
Apollinaire, Guillaume, 32, 93
Aragon, Louis, 31
Ariadne auf Naxos, **122–123**, 139
Arianna's Lament, 74
Arioste, Ludovico, 49
Artaud, Antonin, 224
Astaire, Fred, 153
Auber, Daniel François, 56
Auric, Georges, 113, 173

Bacon, Francis, 93
Bajazet, 67
Ballo in maschera, (Un), 40, 41, 44, 48, 49, 58, **103–104**, 122, 183, 186
Barber of Seville, (The), **93–94**, 170, 173, 178
Barrault, Jean-Louis, 179
Bataille, Henri, 23
Baudelaire, Charles, 81, 127
Beethoven, Ludwig van, 80
Béguin, Albert, 46
Beirer, Hans, 179, 182
Béjart, Maruice, 26, 112

Bel Canto Chronicles, 31

Belle Hélène, (La), 111

Bellini, Vincenzo, 90, 91, 95, 96, 174

Belmonte, Juan, 188, 199

Berg, Alban, 19, 37, 50, 68, 126, 136, 145, 174

Bergonzi, Carlo, 209, 210

Berlioz, Hector, 112, 114

Bertrand, Aloysius, 127

Blake, William, 109

Bohème, (La), 67, 187

Böhm, Karl, 172

Böhme, Kurt, 179

Boito, Arrigo, 112, 114, 117

Boldini, Giovanni, 130

Bolivar, 43, 57, 58

Boris Godounov, 42, 51, 55, 106, 134, 187, 195, 204

Borkh, Inge, 134

Boulez, Pierre, 107, 174

Brecht, Bertolt, 31, 35, 79, 105, 149, 152

Brouwenstijn, Gré, 39

Büchner, Georg, 68, 136, 152

Burlador de Sevilla, (El), 119

Busoni, Ferrucio, 43, 112, 114, 141

Caillois, Roger, 97

Calderón, Pedro, 152

Callas, Maria Meneghini, 91, 132, 191, 198, 202

Calligrammes, 32

Caniglia, Maria, 177

Cantata for the Inauguration of the Museum of Man, 31

231

Capecchi, Renato, 83, 179

Capuletti e i Moticchi, (I), 105

Carmen, 41, 57, 64, 93, 180, 187, 189, 190, 220

Carré, Marguerite, 132

Castel, André, 188

Cavalleria rusticana, 57, 66, 67, 221

Cavalli, Pier Francesco, 77

Cavaradossi, Mario, 130

Chabrier, Emmanuel, 93, 94

Chamberlain, Houston Stewart, 62

Char, René, 75

Charpentier, Gustave, 19, 128

Chekhov, Anton, 20, 152

Chenal, Marthe, 193

Chénier, André, 143, 144

Cherubini, Luigi, 90

Chirico, Georgio de, 55

Christoff, Boris, 198

Cid, (Le), 130

Cilea, Francesco, 57

Clayeux, Louis, 134

Cocteau, Jean, 186

Colonna, Adriano, 105

Comte Ory, (Le), 178

Confessions, (Les), 137

Contes d'Hoffmann, (Les), 41, 187

Coppi, Fausto, 197

Coriolanus, 105

Coronation of Poppaea, 75

Cortis, Marcello, 178, 215

Così fan tutte, 159, 177, 179, 215

Crabbe, George, 121

Da Ponte, Lorenzo, 83

Dali, Salvador, 130

Dame Blanche, (La), 42

Damnation de Faust, (La), 26, **112–113**, 114

Danco, Suzanne, 215

Dangès, Henri, 193, 194

Davy, Gloria, 154

De Quincey, Thomas, 137, 140

Deaf Man's Glance, (The), 156

Dean, James, 191

Death of Rasputin, 56

Debussy, Claude 19, 32, 53, 126, 127, 186, 200

Defoe, Daniel, 209

Delacroix, Eugène, 81

Delmer, Isabel, 133

Desnos, Robert, 31

Dianoluzza, (La), 82

di Marco, Ofelia, 180

Dominguez, Oralia, 75

Don Carlos, 42, 43, 54, 57

Don Giovanni, 24, 27, 37, 41, 45, 49, 60, **83–85**, 158, 178, 179, 186, 204

Don Juan, – see *Don Giovanni*

Don Pasquale, 190

Donizetti, Gaetano, 90, 95, 96

Doré, Gustave, 101

Dottore Faust, (Il), 43, 114

Dreigroschenoper, (Die), – see *The Three Penny Opera*
Duncan, Isadora, 80

Ebert, Carl, 178
Elektra, 50, 136, 196
Eluard, Paul, 74
Emigrant de Landor Road, (L'), 148
Enfant de l'amour, (L'), 23
Erwartung, 20
Eugene Onegin, 187

Fable du fils changé, 43
Falla, Manuel de, 19
Falstaff, 27, 42, 45, 93, 158, 177, 178, 195, 215
Fanciulla del West, (La), 42, 57, 60, 135, 177, 192
Fantômas, 148
Fantomas' Complaint, 31
Faure, Jean-Baptiste, 116
Faust, 41, 50, **114–115**, 187, 194, 195
Femme de Tabarin, (La), 121
Ferrari, Benedetto, 76
Feydeau, Georges, 71
Fidelio, 25, 39, 40, 56, **89,** 172
Fight between Tancredi and Clorinda, (The), 74–76
Filacuridi, Nicola, 213
Fineschi, Onelia, 213
Flaubert, Gustave, 97
Flying Dutchman, (The), 28, 41, 45, 106, 192
Force of Destiny, (The) — see *La Forza del destino*
Fortunes, 31

Forza del destino, (La), 39, 41, 42, 44, 58, 134, 214

Foscari, 49

Four Seasons, (The), 78

Franc-Nohain, 31, 34

Fratre 'nnamorato, (Lo), 214

Freischütz, (Der), 41, 89, 165, 187

Freni, Mirella, 175

Friché, Claire, 193

Gallone, Carmine, 170

Gallupi, Baldassare, 170

Gautier, Théophile, 36

Gay Divorcee, (The), 153

Georg, Stefan, 175

Georgel, 21

Gershwin, George, 49, 154

Gioconda, (La), 42, 187

Giordano, Umberto, 143, 144

Giovanna d'Arco, 44, 48, 197

Girl of the Golden West, (The) – see *La Fanciulla del West*

Giulini, Carlo Maria, 91, 173

Glück, Cristoph Willibald, 112, 117

Gobbi, Tito, 193, 196

Goethe, Johann Wolfgang, 112, 116, 117

Gorky, Maxim, 129

Gounod, Charles, 112, 114

Gozzi, Carlo, 141, 142

Guelfi, Piero, 213

Guglielmo, 158

Guy, Vittorio, 191

Halévy, Ludovic, 34
Hall, Peter, 146
Hamlet, 103, 116, 193
Handel, Georg Friedrich, 79, 81
Hayden, Joseph, 82
Hériodiade, 138, 194
Histoire du soldat, (L'), 22, 43
History of Dramatic Art in France Over the Past 25 Years, 36
Hoffmann, E.T.A., 42, 44, 46, 60, 204
Hugo, Victor, 35, 67, 97, 100, 108
Huguenots, (Les), 52

Igitur, 139
Incoronazione di Poppea, (L'), 75, 76
Indes galantes, (Les), 57
Irma la Douce, 175

Jacob, Max, 31, 34, 109
Jarry, Alfred, 31, 33, 34
Jefta, **79–81**
Joselito, 199
Joseph, 58
Joyaux de la Madone, (Les), 194
Jurinac, Sena, 39

Kipling, Rudyard, 148
Knappertsbusch, Hans, 89
Konnia, Sandor, 176
Kreisleriana, 44, 46

Laforgue, Jules, 138
Lakmé, 57
Lambert, Constant, 133
Lanfang, Mei, 163
Laurens, Claude, 168
Leibowitz, René, 111, 191, 204, 205
Lemaître, Frédérick, 196
Lenin, 128, 129
Lenya, Lotte, 151
Leoncavallo, Ruggiero, 119, 120, 121
Lettera amorosa, 75
Lévi-Strauss, Monique 201
Liang Shanbo and Zhu Yingtai, **157–159**
Limbour, Georges, 31, 93
Livre, (Le), 185
Lohengrin, 45, 176
Loman, Alan, 102
Lorentz, Max, 195
Louise, 31, 67, **128–129**
Loves of Liang Shanbo and Zhu Yingtai, (The), **157–159**
Luce, Claire, 153
Lucia di Lammermoor, 42, **95–96**, 178, 179, 187
Lulu, 43, 50, 136, **145**

Macaire, Robert, 196
Macbeth, 140
Madame Butterfly, 57, 69, **132**, 134, 170, 171, 200, 208, 210
Maeterlinck, Maurice, 24
Magic Flute, (The) — see *Die Zauberflöte*
Magnasco, Alessandro, 100

Mahagonny, **151–152**

Malipiero, Gian Francesco, 43

Mallarmé, Stéphane, 138, 185

Man Who Laughs, (The), 119

Man Who Lost His Shadow, (The), 31

Manelli, Francesco, 76

Manet, Edouard, 93, 98, 116

Manon Lescaut, 144, 208, 209, 210

Marcoux, Vanni, 194

Marriage of Figaro, (The), 40, 50, 84, 97, 183

Marriage of Thetis and Peleus, (The), 77

Marx Brothers, 102

Mascagni, Pietro, 221

Massenet, Jules, 194

Masson, André, 69, 189, 207

Masson, Diego, 171

Maupassant, Guy de, 135

Maurel, Victor, 194

Mavra, 22

Medea, 90

Medium, (The), 42, 155

Mefistofele, 41, 112, 114, **117–118**

Méhul, Etienne, 58

Meilhac, Henri, 34

Meistersinger, (Die), 28, 55, **108**, 187

Melba, Nellie, 95

Mémoires inutiles, 142

Mendès, Catulle, 31, 121

Menotti, Gian Carlo, 155

Mérimée, Prosper, 181

Métraux, Alfred, 166

Meyerbeer, Giacomo, 67, 106

Micaëla (Ofelia di Marco), 180

Mignon, 42, 116

Milhaud, Darius, 31, 227

Milton, John, 109

Mireille, 42

Misérables, (Les), 67, 97

Mister Jelly Roll, 102

Molina, Tirso de, 119

Moll Flanders, 209

Monaco, Mario del, 134, 178, 202

Mondo della luna, (Il), 82

Monteverdi, Claudio, 74, 75, 76, 77

Monzelli, Andrea, 177, 192

Moré, Marcel, 79

Morel, Marisa, 39, 177, 215

Moscucci, Orietta, 210

Moses and Aaron, 23, 50, 58, **146–147**

Mouches, (Les), 54

Mouchoir de nuages, 121

Mozart, Wolfgang Amadeus, 24, 45, 49, 57, 83, 86, 93, 173, 186, 189

Mucha, Alfons, 69

Muette de Portici, (La), 56, 105

Murder as One of the Fine Arts, 137

Mussorgsky, Modest, 157

Nabokov, Vladimir, 56

Nabucco, 42, 58

Nabusco, 49

Nana, 111

Nanteuil, Célestin, 100

Neher, Caspar, 79, 81, 151

Nerval, Gérard de, 31, 54, 167, 185

New Impressions of Africa, 34

Neway, Patricia, 130

Nietzsche, Friedrich, 64, 65

Night at the Opera, (A), 102

Ninfa fidela, (La), **78**

Nobili, Lila de, 98

Norma, **91–92**, 124, 174, 201, 214

Notre Dame de Paris, 67

Nouveau Monde, (Le), 209

Nozze di Figaro — see *The Marriage of Figaro*

Oarsman and the Bozine, (The), 163

Objet aimé, (L'), 33

Offenbach, Jacques, 34, 93, 111

Orfeo — see *Orpheus*

Orphée, 37

Orphée aux enfers, 111

Orpheus, 32, 74, 75, 187

Othello — see *Otello*

Otello, 58, 179, 182, 195

Pabst, Georg Wilhelm, 149

Pagliacci, (I), **119–121**, 135, 159, 171, 196

Paisiello, Giovanni, 94

Paradise Lost, 109

Paradise Regained, 109
Parsifal, 28, 47, 51, 55, 59, 62, **109–110**, 126
Pastori, Antonietta, 191
Patrella, Clara, 210
Pavilion of the West, (The), 163
Pêcheurs de perles, (Les), 57
Pelléas et Mélisande, 24, 53, **126–127**, 173, 186, 189, 200
Pergolese, Jean-Baptiste, 214
Penno, Gino, 204
Penthesilea, 75
Peter Grimes, 103, 187
Philips, Anna, 133
Picasso, Pablo, 18
Piccinni, Niccolo, 46
Pierrot lunaire, 72, 142
Pirandello, Luigi, 43, 121
Plato, 76
Ponchielli, Amilcare, 143
Porgy and Bess, 42, 49, 58, **154**
Porter, Cole, 153
Prêtre, Georges, 130
Prévost, Antoine François (called Abbé) 144, 209
Prophet, 186
Proust, Marcel, 71
Puccini, Giacomo, 19, 46, 60, **69–71**, 72, 74, 124, 127, **133–142**,
    143, 144, 145, 155, 207, 208, 209, 214
Puritane, (I), 42

Queen of Spades, (The), 42

Racine, Jean, 67, 75
Rake's Progress, (The), 43
Ravages of Tobacco, (The), 20, 21
Ravel, Maurice, 19
Renard, Colette, 175
Renaud, Maurice, 192–194
Rienzi, **105**
Rigoletto, 24, 41, 42, 48, 54, 170, 220
Rimbaud, Arthur, 32
Ring of the Nibelung, (The), 55, 61
Rivera, Fermin, 188
Rivière, Georges Henri, 150
Robert le Diable, 42
Roberti, Margherita, 101
Roi s'amuse, (Le), 24, 54
Roméo et Juliette, 42, 187
Rosenkavalier, (Der), 40, 50, 179, 188
Rossi-Lemeni, Nicola 117
Rossini, Gioacchino, 34, 57, 93, 94, 188, 190
Roussel, Raymond, 71, 127
Ruy Blas, 100, 130

Sade, Marquis de, 83
Saint-Pol Roux, 31, 128
Salammbô, 57
Salomé, 25, 41, 50, 58, 136, 185
Santini, Gabriele, 192
Sardou, Victorien, 24
Sartre, Jean-Paul, 54
Satie, Erik, 30, 149

Schiller, Friedrich von, 141

Schoenberg, Arnold, 20, 58, 72, 142, 146, 147

Schwarzkopf, Elizabeth, 199

Schwob, Marcel, 137

Sciutti, Graziella, 178

Scott, Walter, 95

Segalen, Victor, 32

Serafin, Tullio, 91, 134

Serna, Victoriano de la, 188

Shadow, (The), 21

Shakespeare, William, 49, 95, 101, 116, 152, 165

Shattuck, Roger, 33

Siegfried, 28, 50

Sigurd, 193

Sileni, 121

Simionato, Giulietta, 215

Solti, Georg, 183

Somma, Antonio, 49, 183

Somnambula, (La), 42

Song of the Steppe, 57

Spleen de Paris, (Le), 127

Spontini, Gasparo, 90

Stahlmann, Sylvia, 39

Stella, Antonietta, 210

Stendhal, 190

Stich-Randall, Teresa, 175

Strauss, Richard, 19, 50, 58, 122, 124, 135, 139, 185

Stravinsky, Igor, 19, 22, 43, 155, 173

Styx, Lydia, 175

Supervielle, Jules, 31

Sutherland, Joan, 95, 179
Swan Lake, 22
Sylvie, 185

Tagliabue, Carlo, 191
Tannhäuser, 28, 50
Tasso, Torquato, 32, 49
Tebaldi, Renata, 39, 134, **197–198**, 199, 200, 202
Thomas, Ambroise, 116
Three-Penny Opera, (The), 23, 135, 148, 149, 152
Tiepolo, Giandomenico, 209
Todeschi, Elena, 208
Tosca, 24, 56, **130–131**, 136, 170
Toulouse-Lautrec, Henri de, 93
Traviata, (La), 23, 48, 67, **97–99**, 182, 187, 198, 212
Triptyque, (Le), 214
Tristan und Isolde, 28, 42, 53, 55, 59, **107**, 124, 126, 174, 195
Trotsky, Léon, 128, 129
Trovatore, (Il), 27, 42, **100–102**, 170
Turandot, 23, 42, 43, 57, 124, **133–142**, 207
Turn of the Screw, (The), 43
Tzara, Tristan, 121

Verdi, Giuseppe, 19, 27, 35, 42, 44–47, 48, 49, 54, 58, 90, 93,
    97, 103, 106, 116, 117, 122, 157, 186, 189, 197, 222
Verga, Giovanni, 66, 221
Verne, Jules, 127
Vespers for the Virgin Mary, 74, 75
Vestal Virgin, 90
Vie en rose, (La), 209

Visconti, Luigi, 98
Vivaldi, Antonio, 78
von Hofmannsthal, Hugo, 31, 122, 124, 139
von Karajan, Herbert, 200

Wagner, Richard, 28, 37, **44–47**, 53, 55, **59–65**, 105, 106, 108, 110, 117, 124, 126, 173, 186, 189
Wagner, Wieland, 25, 62, 89, 107
War and Peace, 34
Weber, Carl Maria von, 80, 141, 165
Webern, Anton, 175
Wedekind, Frank, 136, 145
Weill, Kurt, 19, 149, 150, 152
White Serpent, (The), 163
Wilhelm Meister's Journeyman Years, 116
Wissman, Lore, 39
Wolf-Ferrari, Ermanno, 180, 194
Woman without a Shadow, (The), **124–125**
Wozzeck, 37, 42, 68, 103, 126, 135, 136, 145, 174, 179, 187

Yu Cheou Fong, 163

Zauberflöte, (Die), 45, 58, 59, 60, **86–88**, 125, 192, 214
Zarevska, Eugenia 175
Zazà, 121
Zeani, Virginia, 178
Zeffirelli, Franco, 95, 96
Zola, Emile, 111, 135

GREEN INTEGER
Pataphysics and Pedantry

Edited by Per Bregne
Douglas Messerli, *Publisher*

Essays, Manifestos, Statements, Speeches, Maxims,
Epistles, Diaristic Notes, Narratives, Natural Histories,
Poems, Plays, Performances, Ramblings, Revelations
and all such ephemera as may appear necessary
to bring society into a slight tremolo of confusion
and fright at least.

*

Green Integer Books

History, or Messages from History Gertrude Stein [1997]
Notes on the Cinematographer Robert Bresson [1997]
The Critic As Artist Oscar Wilde [1997]
Tent Posts Henri Michaux [1997]
Eureka Edgar Allan Poe [1997]
An Interview Jean Renoir [1998]
Mirrors Marcel Cohen [1998]
The Effort to Fall Christopher Spranger [1998]
Radio Dialogs I Arno Schmidt [1999]
Travels Hans Christian Andersen [1999]
In the Mirror of the Eighth King Christopher Middleton [1999]
On Ibsen James Joyce [1999]
Laughter: An Essay on the Meaning of the Comic Henri Bergson [1999]
Operratics Michel Leiris [2001]
Seven Visions Sergei Paradjanov [1998]

Ghost Image Hervé Guibert [1998]
Ballets Without Music, Without Dancers, Without Anything [1999]
Louis-Ferdinand Céline [1999]
My Tired Father Gellu Naum [1999]
Manifestos Manifest Vicente Huidobro [1999]
On Overgrown Paths Knut Hamsun [1999]
What Is Man? Mark Twain [2000]
Metropolis Antonio Porta [1999]
Poems Sappho [1999]
Hell Has No Limits José Donoso [1999]
To Do: A Book of Alphabets and Birthdays
Gertrude Stein [2001]
Letters from Hanusse Joshua Haigh
(edited by Douglas Messerli) [2000]
Theoretical Objects Nick Piombino [1999]
Art *Poetic'* Olivier Cadiot [1999]
Fugitive Suns: Selected Poetry Andrée Chedid [1999]
Mexico. A Play Gertrude Stein [2000]
Sky-Eclipse: Selected Poems Régis Bonvicino [2000]
The Twofold Vibration Raymond Federman [2000]
The Antiphon Djuna Barnes [2000]
The Resurrection of Lady Lester OyamO [2000]
Crowtet I: A Murder of Crows and *The Hyacinth Macaw*
Mac Wellman [2000]
Hercules Richelieu and *Nostradamus* Paul Snoek [2000]
Abingdon Square María Irene Fornes [2000]
The Masses Are Asses Pedro Pietri [2000]
*Three Masterpieces of Cuban Drama: Plays by Julio Matas,
Carlos Felipe, and Virgilio Piñera* edited with an Introduction
by Luis F. González-Cruz and Ann Waggoner Aken [2000]
Rectification of Eros Sam Eisenstein [2000]
Drifting Dominic Cheung (Chang Ts'o) [2000]

Green Integer EL-E-PHANT Books
[6 x 9 format]

The PIP Anthology of World Poetry of the 20th Century 1 [2000]
edited with a Preface by Douglas Messerli
readiness / enough / depends / on Larry Eigner [2000]

BOOKS FORTHCOMING FROM GREEN INTEGER

Islands and Other Essays Jean Grenier
The Doll and *The Doll at Play* Hans Bellmer
[with poetry by Paul Éluard]
American Notes Charles Dickens
Prefaces and Essays on Poetry
William Wordsworth
Confessions of an English Opium-Eater
Thomas De Quincey
The Renaissance Walter Pater
Venusburg Anthony Powell
Captain Nemo's Library Per Olav Enquist
Selected Poems and Journal Fragments Maurice Gilliams
Utah Toby Olson
The Pretext Rae Armantrout
Gold Fools Gilbert Sorrentino
Against Nature J. K. Huysmans
Satyricon Petronius [translation ascribed to Oscar Wilde]
The Cape of Good Hope Emmanuel Hocquard
Traveling through Brittany Gustave Flaubert
Delirum of Interpretations Fiona Templeton